Recipes for Conversation

A Guide to
Hosting Authentic Conversations
in the Digital Age
(and a Pandemic)

Pat Montandon

Recipes for Conversation:
A Guide to Hosting Authentic Conversations in the Digital Age (and a Pandemic)
By Pat Montandon

ISBN-13: 978-1-0879-3054-1 (hardcover)

Cover illustration: Aron Kincaid
Book design: Future Studio Los Angeles

patmontandon.com

Printed in U.S.

DEDICATED TO

Owen Wilsey
Mira Annapurna Wilsey
Cristina Korzon

Contents

Transcripts from the Roundtable

The purpose of
Recipes for Conversation
is threefold:

1 *Recipes* champions for a return to meaningful conversation. In the digital age, people talk but they seldom listen. We talk to each other online, on our smart phones, via text messages, Snapchat, Instagram, and Facebook. We watch people talk on our favorite reality shows and feel part of the conversation while we tweet about what we're seeing and hearing. The problem, of course, is that this means we mostly talk *AT* each other rather than *WITH* each other, face to face. *Recipes for Conversation* advocates creating intimate gatherings that start with a topic of conversation, but quickly become something much more satisfying in a world that seems to be growing ever more distant and uncaring.

2 *Recipes* encourages readers to seek out people whom they admire or are curious about, and to feel comfortable hosting strangers in their home. It provides practical advice about how to approach potential guests and create a group that will spark lively, enriching, and astonishing conversation.

3 Included are transcripts and photographs from Roundtables, providing a fascinating snapshot of my various guests as well as a window into past eras of America's history.

CHAPTER ONE

Recipes for Conversation

Shirley Temple was the magical tap-dancing princess of my impoverished childhood in Waurika, Oklahoma, a vision of unimaginable glamour. I wanted all things Shirley Temple—from coloring books to dolls. When my pious mother refused to indulge me, I was heartbroken. "Patsy Lou," she said, "you know it's a sin to go to the movies, and even if it wasn't we don't have money for such frivolity!" So you can imagine how excited I was, several decades later, when the real-life Shirley Temple (Black) was my guest at a Roundtable luncheon! There she was, from the silver screen to my table! And so it goes at the Roundtable.

Growing up in Oklahoma during the Dust Bowl and the Great Depression I learned firsthand about scrimping and looking for bargains. Despite our meager dinners, my family had a Roundtable supper once a week or so—although they didn't call it a Roundtable, they called it, "getting people together to talk."

My father, being a true minister of the people, met folk from all walks of life and would often invite them to dine with us. The mix made for fascinating conversation. They were a collection of disparate folks—a down-on-his-luck bum, a missionary from Africa, a Fuller Brush salesman, a neighbor couple, the mayor, a suffragette—all gathered at our large round dining table, everyone equal, eating, talking, laughing, and occasionally, crying as we bared our souls in an honest and forthright way.

My father (who was also a Father of the Nazarene church,

and so a father to me twice-
over!) would say a prayer, blessing the humble meal for the
nourishment of our bodies and
then guests helped themselves
to bowls of steaming red beans,
collard greens, cornbread and
onions. Daddy would ask a question and the conversation began
to flow like that river of milk and

*No one
condemned the
man's views
or tried to
convert him,
and we enjoyed
his tales of an
unstructured life.*

honey he preached about. The talk wasn't always silky and sweet,
sometimes it was more like firecrackers going down the gullet, but
it was always interesting.

"Brother James," my father said to the homeless man in our
dining room, "why are you so down-on-your-luck? What happened to pull you off the railroad tracks of life?

"Well, Reverend," the man said between big gulps of butter-
milk, "I'm not a Christian, so accordin' to your Bible I'm not a be-
liever. But, you know, sir, I kinda like ridin' the rails, not havin' a
care in the world, seein' the countryside and sleepin' in ditches."

"'Cept when it's raining, I betcha," my sixteen-year-old brother, Charles, chimed in, prompting laughter from the adults.

"No, not then," James said with a snaggle-toothed grin, "Then
I wrap myself up in oil cloth and try to find a dry barn somewheres
to sleep inside of."

No one condemned the man's views or tried to convert him, and
we enjoyed his tales of an unstructured life. The same was true of
the missionary who regaled us with stories about elephants and li-
ons and monkeys, as well as saving souls in Africa. Looking back, I
wish we had talked about marriage and the trials and tribulations
of relationships—subjects we have no trouble talking about today.

After a twelve-year marriage I pulled up stakes and moved to
California. During a year-long stint in a UC Hospital I fell in love
with San Francisco, the city "air conditioned by God." At that time,

I was living on a ranch in the San Joaquin Valley, a rice-growing region in central California. After undergoing heart surgery as the tenth patient in the world to survive it, and after years of moving from one place to another with my husband, we divorced. I was young and foolish and didn't know to ask for alimony, and drove to San Francisco in a secondhand purple-and-white Chrysler with only four hundred dollars to my name.

The first thing I did was to find an apartment and a job. It wasn't difficult to solve those problems. I had experience in the retail world so that was a good place to start. But then I fell into a deep well of loneliness. I had no friends. As much as I longed to be invited to one of the shindigs I read about in the *San Francisco Chronicle*, I knew it would never happen if I stayed on the same trajectory as my old Chrysler. I remembered the Sunday Suppers my parents held when I was a child. Why, I could do the same thing, I realized. Then I thought of the poem *"Outwitted"* by Edwin Markham, that I'd memorized as a girl:

> *They drew a circle that shut me out,*
> *Heretic, rebel, a thing to flout.*
> *But love and I had the wit to win*
> *We drew a circle that took them in*

So, you know what I did? I decided to grow my circle by inviting people to my apartment for lunch or supper, and soon my friendships grew like blossoms in springtime. A reporter and photographer for *The San Francisco Chronicle* attended one of my parties (at a time when newspapers were our main source of information long before Social Media was a gleam in Mark Zuckerberg's eye) and soon a large feature about my Roundtable—complete with photographs—appeared in the Sunday paper. Not long after that, reporters from other news

I decided to grow my circle by inviting people to my apartment for lunch or supper

*Laugh with me at my mistakes,
learn from my victories,
and reap the amazing rewards of
relating to people on a level you
may never have thought possible.*

agencies were clamoring to attend my get-togethers and I became a San Francisco "celebrity". Doors opened for me everywhere. McGraw-Hill offered me a contract to write a book on how to be a hostess and it wasn't long before I had a job hosting a TV show on KGO (the local ABC affiliate), called *Pat's Prize Movie*. I had thirty minutes of "talk time" and an hour for an old film. These were the early days of television and I was on my own, allowed to choose whatever topic I could think of. It was great fun.

When my first book, *How To Be a Party Girl* was published in 1965 noted San Francisco columnist Herb Caen reported, "Pat's book took longer to gestate than that of an elephant!" If Herb were around today, he would have plenty to say about the time it has taken me to write *Recipes for Conversation*. After 30 years of hosting Roundtable luncheons and Sunday suppers—some 500 well-attended scintillating meals—ta da!—Here it is!

The steps I took to escape the lonely routine of my life and bring the party to my dining room are contained in this book. My life became enriched and is the reason I happily share this information with you. Laugh with me at my mistakes, learn from my victories, and reap the amazing rewards of relating to people on a level you may never have thought possible.

PREPARING THE SCENE

After ten years in San Francisco I remarried, and my husband and I lived in a penthouse overlooking the Bay. We were known for our A-list parties. Still, I had begun yearning for conversations that went beyond chitchat about the weather, who wore what to the opera, etc. I was hungry to have conversations with people from different walks of life whose choices, circumstances, and accomplishments were polar opposites of mine.

The incubator for heart-felt conversation does not exist at most social functions; I felt emptier when I left a party than when I arrived. For my emotional well being, I needed to form connections with people beyond my social circle with whom I could communicate on a deep, honest level.

I'm not going to lie; when I first started out, I feared that I wasn't up to the task of creating a Salon. While I was confident that I could handle invitations, food, service, and introductions, I wondered if I'd be able to set the tone for the kind of conversations I was seeking. Could I lead such a conversation, keep it going, and unsnarl it if necessary? I didn't feel totally secure in my ability to avoid possible disasters—ugly disagreements, awkward silences— and keep the talk flowing smoothly in productive directions.

My plan for the Roundtables meant that many of my guests would be strangers to me—some shy, some overbearing, some accomplished and knowledgeable in fields I knew nothing about. Almost all of them would certainly have more formal education than I did; all I had was a high school diploma and six months of college.

Despite my fears, my first gathering was a success. My longtime friend, Merla Zellerbach, encouraged me to turn my knowledge into a book and *Recipes for Conversation* was born. She was as hungry for substantial interactions as much as I was. "I am sick of meaningless talk." Merla said. "Most social events remind me of the inane questions asked celebrities at awards shows. 'Who are you wearing?' 'Do you think the Crockers are getting a divorce?' 'Oh, look at that ugly centerpiece! Who uses sunflowers?'" Gossip is not food for the soul.

At the Roundtable we talk about things like rape, racism, and how to make the world a better place. We put our phones to bed; I have a docking system where guests charge their cellphones out of sight of the table. I devised The Question, asked towards the end of each luncheon. We also honed our listening skills, interpreting body language and thoughtful inquiries until we were comfortable asking and answering profoundly personal questions.

OUR STORIES AND OUR FRIENDS

Too often we hide from the stories that define us. Perhaps we think we need to fabricate our days, hoping to appear more important than we feel we are. But I've found, after decades of bringing strangers together, that people are eager for an honest setting in which they can reveal their raw and unpretentious selves.

At one of my luncheons in 1978 for example, the legendary concert promoter Bill Graham told us about coming to America from Germany as a child.

His decidedly Brooklyn accent would have convinced you that he was a native English speaker. "My parents sent me and my siblings out of Germany, away from the Nazis, when it became obvious that as Jews we were in danger. We were split up: some were sent to China, others to Russia. I was sent to New York in September of '41 and three months later, the war broke out between Germany and America. I became a doorstep-child. Strangers took me in. The kids here didn't care what your religion was. If you spoke German, you were a Nazi. So I got my head kicked in going to and from school every day. I never spoke German again until after my success as a musical wizard. I found my siblings from all across the world and brought them to the top-of-the-hill mansion I built in California's Marine County. We stood around the piano singing the old German songs of our childhood for the first time . . . ." Bill's sobs resonated around the table, as tears of sympathy ran down the cheeks of all those seated there that day. Like Bill, we used napkins to wipe our faces. It was a true Roundtable moment of honesty and heart.

At another luncheon the author of the sensational best seller *Roots*, Alex Haley, told of the impact the *Roots* miniseries (which aired in 1977) had on his life. "Everything was pretty quiet, even

when Roots as a book was just running away. And then the television show played. On the last night of the show, when 80 million
people were watching, I came on for the last four minutes. That
was it. But the next morning when I got out of the cab at Kennedy
Airport to catch the plane for Los Angeles, I was mobbed."

Such are the fascinating and bonding personal stories, that
spill out at the Roundtable. Some of the guests I remember most
fondly weren't well known at all. There was Shirley Boccaccio, an
attractive dark haired, single mother of three small children. Shirley was on welfare and talked about her view of herself. She gave
the rest of us an insight into the trials of those struggling with pov-
erty. Later, Shirley published books for children and happily left
the welfare rolls.

Another woman at a Roundtable revealed she had been oper-
ated on for a malignant brain tumor. "When I learned I could die
soon, it changed my whole concept of life. Life became so valuable.
I now live for each minute and find great pleasure in the most simple task." Her words prompted a lengthy conversation about life
and death and what we each wanted before we took our last breath.

Inez Garcia, another guest, was out of jail on bail. Born in a
New York ghetto, she could neither read nor write. During a highly emotional moment, Inez, who was extremely articulate, told us
about killing the man who had raped her. By the time she finished
talking, we were convinced of her lack of guilt and many of the
guests volunteered to support her cause and help pay for her defense. We were gratified later, when a judge declared her innocent.

Rape was also the subject at the following 1976 Roundtable.

... when I was in San Quentin, and then thereafter,

GUESTS

◄ **Eldridge Cleaver** • An American writer and political activist; a prominent member of the Black Panthers and held the titles of Minister of Information and Head of the International Section of the Panthers

Merla Zellerbach • San Francisco philanthropist socialite founded SF Sponsors and Conard House for mental health

Dr. Rollo May • Psychologist, author of *Love and Will* (1969) a major proponent of existential psychotherapy ►

Marcia Brandwynne • Los Angeles news anchor

Sydney Goldstein • Founder of City Arts & Lectures in San Francisco

Mimi Silbert • Founder of Delancey Street Foundation provides ex-felons, prostitutes, substance abusers, and others with academic and social skills

Father Miles Riley • Catholic priest, television and radio personality

... it just ate me up because there was no way I could justify what I had done.

DIALOG FROM A ROUNDTABLE

ELDRIDGE: *The only time I ever did anything that I felt guilty about was rape. And I didn't get caught for it. But it was just something that ate me up.*

MERLA: *What was your motivation for rape?*

ELDRIDGE: *I still have difficulty in ironing that out. The way it happened the first time—I was living with a girl in an apartment in Los Angeles and we had to spend a couple of days in a motel while the apartment was painted. Well, we were sitting in the car outside this motel waiting for our room to come up and the girl with me saw her next-door neighbor, who was a married man, going into this motel with a girl who wasn't his wife. She called to him and he came over to the car and pleaded with her not to tell anybody. And I just had a big flash on the vulnerability of people who go to motels. There is a whole scene that's going on that can't be reported, nine times out of ten. I was on parole and I had been selling marijuana and I had this big wad of money on me. If somebody had robbed me, I couldn't have done anything. So anyway, the next weekend I found myself back at the same motel.*

SYDNEY: *Why?*

ELDRIDGE: *Because I saw that these people could be ripped off with impunity. So I went back to do it. I followed a couple into a motel room and I tied the guy up and put him in the closet and did what he had come there to do. And it wasn't reported. There was something about the motel situation that intrigued me, pulled me. I wrote a poem about motels. To me, a motel was like an obscene institution, you know? I kept going back, every weekend to that motel and others.*

But, years later, when I was in San Quentin, and then thereafter, it just ate me up because there was no way I could justify what I had done. It just kept coming back to me as something wrong. No problem with robbing a Safeway store, which I had also done. I was glad about that, you know. But this particular act—rape—it just drove me up the wall.

MARCIA: *But when you did these things, when criminals rape and rob—aren't they afraid of getting caught, of being put in jail, of their freedom being taken away?*

MIMI: *Most of the people going around committing crimes really have no freedom to lose.*

ELDRIDGE: *You don't calculate that far. The act itself is what you want to accomplish. Most criminals don't really plan their retreat, you know, like how to get out of a bank after you get the money and the cops are coming. The guy may feel that if he didn't get killed he got off lightly, you know? And you have to distinguish between crimes against property and crimes against the person.*

ROLLO: *That's what rape is.*

ELDRIDGE: *If a guy goes after property there's sort of a cold-blooded calculation involved. He's weighed the risk and he's weighed the gains, even to the extent of saying, "If I get this money and get away with it, great. But if I get caught—" Then he calculates the number of hours that he will spend in jail. And often they equate with the number of hours he would have had to work for the same amount. I used to do it all the time.*

MIMI: *And it's better in jail almost, than some of the jobs.*

FR. MILES: *Plus, it's a crapshoot. You still have a chance of getting off scot-free.*

SYDNEY: *I think this about life—that everyone wants to feel a sense of power over their lives and a sense of control and most people don't. Committing crimes is a temporary surge of power. Rape certainly is. And research on this shows that women who become extremely aggressive rather than being the victim, who* *begin to take sexual initiative, then——.*

MIMI: *The rapist wilts and goes away?*

MERLA: *I've wondered about that. What would happen if you say 'this is fabulous, where have you been all my life?'*

PAT: *It would be a very unusual woman who could do that.*

MARCIA: *If anybody could have done that it would have been Carolyn Craven. But she said she couldn't when it happened to her because she felt if the man could rape, he could kill.*

MERLA: *And also he kept saying, 'Pretend you enjoy it,' which is kind of weird.*

ROLLO: *Who said this, the rapist?*

MARCIA: *Yes, this guy who has committed seventy known rapes in Berkeley. And he just happened to hit on a reporter, Carolyn Craven, of Channel 9.*

FR. MILES: *She was really gutsy.*

MARCIA: *He threatened his victims that if they reported him he would come back and kill them, but she had the courage to go public.*

ELDRIDGE: *Do you think he chose her or was it random?*

MARCIA: *He doesn't know who the women are, but he watches their pattern for about five days and knows how they live. He has never chosen a house with a dog in it, or a house with a husband or a male who is there regularly. It's always a woman alone or a woman with a child.*

ROLLO: *Is he still at large?*

PAT: *Yes. It's been headlined in the papers. Rollo doesn't watch TV or read the papers.*

ROLLO: *Only the* New York Times.

... if we have a society that depends solely on the penal code and the policeman, then everything is already lost.

ELDRIDGE: *I just want to point out something I am more and more impressed with as time goes by. That is, we have become more and more preoccupied with the penal code and the civil code. But there are other codes that really preceded these two. These are codes that are not policed by policemen but by family and community and self. And if we have a society that depends solely on the penal code and the policeman, then everything is already lost.*

MERLA: *You're right.*

ELDRIDGE: *It's really the policeman of the heart.*

Don't think for a second after reading these topics of conversation that we are always serious. *No Lordy, no!* At one luncheon we spent the entire three hours laughing. Every time a heavy topic began another person would interject a story that had us helpless with mirth. Inyoung Boyd, originally from Korea, told us about reading *Gone With The Wind*, and was seized with the desire to become Scarlett O'Hara. This beautiful Korean woman envisioning herself as a Southern Belle in hoop skirts brought peals of laughter to the table. That wasn't all; Inyoung left Korea and flew to Atlanta, Georgia intent on becoming a true Southerner. She opened a store for Korean foods in a city that had no interest in such foreign delicacies. "They wanted fried everything, even fried ice cream," she reported.

As you can imagine, because I live in Hollywood, the talk some-times veers to celebrities. Guest Bob Ellison, a writer on the icon-ic *Mary Tyler Moore Show*, talked about touring Michael Cage's

They were a collection of disparate folks—a down-on-his-luck bum, a missionary from Africa, a Fuller Brush salesman, a neighbor couple, the mayor, a suffragette—all gathered at our large round dining table, everyone equal, eating, talking, laughing, and occasionally, crying as we bared our souls in an honest and forthright way.

Bel-Air Tudor mansion—formerly owned by Dean Martin and later Tom Jones. "You should have seen the place," Bob said, leaning back in his chair, "the Olympic size pool was a mess, actually a swamp! Full of tree branches, debris, and filthy water. I looked at that mess and said—"Hey Michael, you must use the same pool boy as I do."

Everyone longs for meaningful connections with other humans. Over the long years of my life, I have learned that people who lack them fill up the resulting void in different ways. Some people become alcoholics, some become religious zealots, or thieves, or lovers. There are as many ways to cope, as there are causes of pain. We need to be able to talk with forthright honesty about our most deeply felt desires and voice our opinions without fear. Once in a while, we even feel compelled to cry in the company of others, without embarrassment. The ability to laugh at the silly things we have done without fear of censure is a gift. We need real camaraderie.

CHAPTER TWO

Call Waiting?

The need to deeply connect with other people is a human need, not a generational one; thirty-something's are as eager to convey their inner most thoughts and experiences as people in their 20s, 60s, and all ages above and below. It's not about age; it's about engagement with others on a visceral level.

Perhaps you are a natural born party-planner. If so, well, hooray for you, darling'. Go for it! If you are a loyal lifer to a group of friends and always pal around with them then meeting new people might be a challenge. Maybe you know each other so well you're like the old joke about the guys who had been in prison together so long they only had to shout out a number to get a laugh. If that's true then you might be growing dull and boring without being aware of it. So stop shouting out a number and get out there and GROW! I'll give you an outline to help make that happen and a shoulder to cry on, should you need it.

More than two billion people visit Facebook every single day. When I heard this, I decided to change. I limit my online time to one day a week. Think about what that means: 1 day a week = 52 weeks a year = 416 hours= 2,080 hours in 5 years or 260 weeks, or, help me out here I've gone as far as I can with this math quiz. What I do know off the top of my head is that this is plenty of time to connect with old friends, new friends, and even people with whom I might not want to talk if I met them in person.

It's terrific to have friends from Beijing to Moscow and catching up with them is easy today. The hard part is that even though we send emails and see their photos on Facebook, we still haven't really caught up with them, in the true sense of the word. We haven't seen the look in their eyes, a telltale tear, or a hint of a smile. There is no substitute for the warmth of a big hug in real time, a kiss on the cheek (or on the lips if you're so inclined) rather than the cold feel of a mouse. Cyberspace is great, but I'll take a real meal with flesh and blood human beings over the empty feeling of downing a bowl of soup while chatting via Skype. Buddies from high school can quench your curiosity. But do you know the people who live next door? You would if your house burned down, but I hope it doesn't come to that before you introduce yourself. Borrow that proverbial cup of sugar and exchange greetings. So, lay down your smartphone, take your hands off the keyboard and quickly step away from your computer.

Learning how to create heart-to-heart dialogue while breaking bread together is a time-honored custom. And it doesn't have to cost much, either.

Don't panic, it won't hurt. By taking this advice you won't even miss that robotic ping of notifications on your device when someone responds to a tweet because you will be saying "I've got friends, *real friends* whom I know on a deep level, just as they know me." I'm not suggesting that you give up your computer, Heavens NO—I love my computer and e-mail and all that good Internet stuff, but it's not my LIFE. Nor should it be your life. If it is, you are missing out on fun and connections that matter. You could also be missing out on romance and love. Are you ready to take the plunge? Okay, let's go...

Hosting a Roundtable Salon is worth any effort you may put into it. Trust me. It's true. Learning how to create heart-to-heart dialogue while breaking bread together is a time-honored custom. And it doesn't have to cost much, either. Most of us are concerned

Another Opening, Another Show

1. Clear your calendar in advance – no need to plan a perfect party, only to have the cable guy show up somewhere between 9:00 AM and never o'clock. Of course, should that happen, you could always invite him or her to sit down and join in the discussion. They would probably enjoy a good meal too.

2. Go over your guest list and then send out your e-mail invitations. By acting quickly you are more likely to have the first guests you invite say yes.

3. Be sure to have an RSVP date on the bottom of the invitation. If an invitee can't make it then you have time to invite another guest.

4. Before doing anything else and after selecting a date review these tips to see what works best for you. Nothing is chiseled in marble. These pages contain the blueprint, but the rest is up to you.

about money in this time of economic trials. I know about that and will give you alternative menus in chapter seven.

YOU'VE GOT A FRIEND IN ME

Before putting a guest list together you need to think about inviting a friend to be your Party Buddy. Select someone you know and like and ask yourself lots of questions about this individual before you invite them to be part of this amazing experience. You need a person you can depend on.

Be wholly honest in your evaluation. We always want to see only the best in our friends, which is a good thing, but you need a friend with a proven record to be your Roundtable Buddy. Go for it, darlin'! I'm with you all the way!

Your helper must be aware of the world around them, able to comment on topics ranging from racial strife to global warming to conflicts in the Middle East to Hollywood (a big topic for some and kind of fun, too). Can you and your Buddy converse on these topics should they come up in conversation? I don't mean that you should suddenly become Christiane Amanpour giving a report on CNN, but if you know a little about a subject you will feel more comfortable and you'll learn a lot too.

Remember, as host you are in charge and you can steer the conversation to whatever topic you choose. How to do that is for a later chapter. Right now we need to help you select a Roundtable Buddy, explain why you need one, and make you comfortable through the whole process. Please don't misunderstand; I'm not suggesting you want a jump-up-and-down giggling sort of buddy, heaven forbid. I feel jangled just thinking about them. No, you want someone who knows how to enjoy the Roundtable/Party experience with you, will support you, and is somewhat levelheaded.

If you're shy by nature, choose a friend with whom you are at ease, a friend who will help you be the fabulous host you were meant to be. There are good-energy, bad-energy, and no-energy humans. Given a choice—and you will need to think this through—I would select a show-hog or drama queen over a no-energy drip or a bore. Your secret weapon will be a friend with a sense of humor, someone who can laugh at herself just as you can. This is a crucial gift for you and anyone who wants to become the "Hostess with the Mostest." Give it some thought and then go with your gut. I'll bet someone immediately comes to mind. Go! Now! Don't waste a minute. Get that angel on the phone!

FOOD, GLORIOUS FOOD

Once you have someone to help you, invite your party buddy to an afternoon at the Farmers Market or gourmet grocers. Prowl around and survey the color, texture, and taste of the food. What colors will pop on the plate and what looks appetizing?

I was once invited to dinner at the home of a friend who served cod, mashed potatoes, and cauliflower—all dull shades of white. Then to make her food appear even more unappetizing it was served on a white platter. It looked like prison chow! I wondered what we were being punished for. An unattractive representation

---

Trust in Me, Darlin', Oh Trust in Me. Trust but Verify

1. Does your Buddy keep their word?

2. If you ask for a favor do they help you? Or explain why they can't?

3. Are they fun to be around?

4. Do they laugh out loud?

5. Do you enjoy their company?

6. Do they have positive energy?

7. Do they know their way around a kitchen?

8. Are they comfortable talking to strangers?

9. Lastly: Does your Party Buddy keep up with current events? (Gosh, that sounds like a class from high school doesn't it?

... keep the menu simple.
Get advice from the people who work at your local market, what pairs well with what and perhaps they can point you in the direction of their favorite condiments, sauces, and spreads.

like that one can sabotage conversation faster than President Bush Sr. did when he threw up on the Japanese Prime Minister. (Yes, that really happened!)

Together with your buddy, make a few sample menus of potential starters and mains that compliment one another along with a shopping list and prep list of things to do.

To narrow down the possibilities, keep the menu simple. Get advice from the people who work at your local market, what pairs well with what and perhaps they can point you in the direction of their favorite condiments, sauces, and spreads. Those foodies are passionate and hold a wealth of information; you might even recruit one as a new Roundtable guest. Remember, food that is in season costs less and tastes better so with that said, keep the time of year in mind when menu planning. I love a thick, spicy chili, but a heavy stew in summer or a light salad in February, are not appealing. Get those wheels turning to concoct themes for your meal —Italian, comfort food, maybe a grilled lunch—or work around the signature dishes you make really well. Graduate from scrambled eggs and spaghetti, darlin', show your skills! There are so many great cookbooks that can guide you all the way, such as *The Barefoot Contessa Cookbook* by Ina Garten (1999), *Milk Street: The New Rules – Recipes That Will Change The Way You Cook* by Christopher Kimball (2019), and *The Bon Appetit Cookbook* by Barbra Fairchild (2006). *The Bon Appetit Cookbook* has everything in it that you could want to know about cooking, and is a book you should have in your library in any case!

The mother of a friend isn't much of a cook, but she does

pirogue's (Polish dumplings stuffed with mashed potato and cheese) really well so at every gathering, and I mean *every* gathering, she pulls out the pirogue pan and the crowd goes wild. When you decide what you are serving, even if it's an old standard, plan a test of your meal prior to the lunch with a few friends. This will make a big difference in terms of the timing, what tools you need and how the dish turns out when made in a larger quantity.

PEOPLE WHO NEED PEOPLE

When planning your luncheon, you should keep a pen and notebook in your purse, heck, even beside your bed. After all, bright ideas can hit at any time. Start by jotting down the names of people you would like to invite, people you'd like to know better, people you enjoy, and people who would spark off of one another. Don't underestimate the power of fireworks across the table as ideas are put forth. Don't get all flustered and bothered should that happen. It's not up to you to pour oil on seething waters. These people are adults and if they feel comfortable enough to let the fur fly, well great. Let it happen. Your guests will jump in and have their say, too. That's all to the good. Didn't I tell you to not under any circumstances be boring? Stay calm, though. Don't be shy about voicing your opinions, either.

At a Roundtable some years ago the mayor of San Jose arrived late and she was obviously unsettled. She explained that she had just left a city council meeting about the right of gays to have a parade. Janet Gray Hayes had sided with the gay rights people and was so harassed about her opinion that she fled to the restroom to regain her composure. As she began to recount her ordeal she started to cry which prompted another guest to accuse her of being soft, "that's the problem with women in power, they cry

These people are adults and if they feel comfortable enough to let the fur fly, well great. Let it happen.

instead of being tough . . . etc." Well the whole table got into the mix and one guest even blotted Janet's tears with a napkin. You can read the transcript in chapter eight. Photos of that dramatic luncheon are also there. It was a remarkable exchange and one that proves our point of not trying to stifle a heated discussion. As you will read the argument ended in a way that would challenge even the most gifted novelist.

When making your list of those to invite think about the chatty grocery clerk with the intricate tattoos, the personal trainer at your gym who was a former Marine. Anyone you've chatted with who doesn't seem like an axe-murderer has potential. Step out of your bubble; you can't get a YES if you don't ask. You might want to have a regular rotation of friends with whom you pal around at social functions. By all means extend an invitation to two or three of them. But be aware that no one likes being the odd woman out at a table of BFF's cracking inside jokes, so aim for balance between new acquaintances and those whose faces are familiar.

> *Anyone you've chatted with who doesn't seem like an axe-murderer has potential.*

You might have 874 "friends" on Facebook, but think about connecting with folks the old-fashioned way, face-to-face over a great meal. Ah, the good old days! Somewhere along the way it became way too easy to connect to everyone we've ever known in this life and maybe beyond. In the process though, we distanced ourselves from the people around us. Studies by Dr. Robin Dunbar (a University of Oxford anthropologist and evolutionary psychologist) have shown that the brain can effectively process only 150 friends. After that they get jumbled in a blur, and who wants to be a blur?

The purpose of the Roundtable is to create an environment wherein conversation moves easily between strangers in a safe environment where real connections can evolve. It's up to you to make your guests feel safe to open up. At the beginning of lunch, tell everyone that the Roundtable is a place for open discussions about whatever subject comes up and that it's important to keep the conversations in confidence, not to reveal the secrets divulged at the Roundtable. Think seriously about how to word what you say in order to have the confidence of those present. Be sure to enlist the support of your Party Buddy and your group of rotating members in your effort to generate a safe environment for Real... not artificial ... Talk!

It's important to invite people of varying ages, ethnic groups, occupations, and interests to your luncheon. Trust me. Contrasts incite passion, adrenaline, emotions, and maybe even tears. These ingredients create the quality conversation we're seeking. Having people with differing and strong opinions at the same table creates an opportunity to hear both sides of an issue. We tend to flock in circles of the likeminded, like geese flying south for the winter. But people with varied political or religious viewpoints can have a surprising number of things in common and we can learn a lot from listening and commenting as issues unfold. How boring to be at a gathering where everyone thinks alike. Great, we all agree, pass the salt. Yawn! A memorable Roundtable allows you a chance to experience the whole person and not define them based on who you think they are or judge them by the neighborhood in which they live, or the way they are dressed.

At one luncheon Father Miles Riley, who had recently been mugged and beaten was on crutches. Another guest was Eldridge Cleaver who had raped and robbed people. Eldridge had committed these crimes years prior and had served a lengthy prison sentence before returning to society. At the Roundtable, both men openly shared their experiences as victim and violator, while exposing their individual process of rehabilitation and healing. With the permission of my visitors I recorded that conversation and can share it with you. Fascinating!

I like having my Roundtable luncheons on a Sunday at 12:30 P.M. But you know your community and therefore, need to select a day and time that works best for you and your friends. For many, Sunday is family day but usually a spouse can get away for a Sunday afternoon every once in a while. Now this is where your persuasive charm comes to play. Pour it on darlin' because it's important! If at all possible, do not invite couples to your Roundtable. Why? People tend to open up when their significant other is not present which is what you want. Perfect example. At a recent luncheon, the subject turned to sex, whirlwind romances, and rape. Interestingly, the males were open about the subject but the females pulled an Elmer Fudd and it got "Veeewy veeewy qwiiiiet." When it comes to couples, you are dealing with a complex situation where people have a code of conduct when others enter their bubble, as well as having secrets they may want to keep from each other. We want to know the individual, who they are without the title of Mrs, Mom, or John Q. Husband. Assure your friend that their spouse is on your list for a future luncheon.

INVITE ME IN

When you're satisfied with the final names, ask your Party Buddy to review your guest list and assess the notes you jotted down. To ensure that everyone has a chance to talk, limit your guest list to six or eight or at the *most* ten people. Remember, your focus is on conversation, so keep it manageable. Send out your invitations two weeks in advance of the date. Evite.com is a fantastic tool or type up your own invitation. Keep the template classic. The tone for lunch is mindfulness, not a luau happy hour—that's another party all together! Plan and prepare for a three-hour lunch. However, I once had a lunch that lasted seven hours! Yes, I did. Finally,

A way to sow the seeds of conversation is to research some "hot topics" or take time for introspection while thinking about deeper subjects.

I suggested it was time for my guests to leave, but that experience just proved how hungry people are for good conversation and their reluctance to leave it! When you get involved in good conversation, full of laughter and honesty, time flows faster than a Jamaican sprinter at the Olympics. It happens every time! And though you may have a gorgeous garden, mosquitoes, traffic, and the tricky logistics of serving outdoors can distract from the dialogue.

A way to sow the seeds of conversation is to research "hot topics" or take time for introspection while thinking about deeper subjects. Is there a controversy happening in your city, a scandal that is on everyone's lips? A government issue that's gone amok?

Some example questions to consider:

- *When were you the happiest?*
- *Was there a sad moment in your childhood that still influences you?*
- *What causes your heart to beat faster, other than exercise and sex, of course?*

WHO ARE YOU, DARLIN'?

Along with the invitation, request a short biography including personal notes and hobbies/interests. Set the tone by writing your own bio to send out so your guests will know something about you. It should not be lengthy—you're not writing the great American novel—but it should be informative. After the bios come trickling in, compile them into a single document, and send them out to your guests. Crucial: Be sure you read the bios. This will help immensely with icebreakers and where to seat your guests. Does the former prostitute sit beside the PTA president? Sure, why not? Father Miles Riley and Eldridge Cleaver prove the benefits of an unconventional seating arrangement. In the later part of this book, you will read transcripts of lunches, all with their different dynamics. Mix it up, really, get to know people you probably would ordinarily never meet under different circumstances. Do not be judgmental. You will learn something you otherwise would never know.

GO FOR IT, I SAY

And of course, I do not want to ignore the titillating possibility of romance. You have an opportunity to invite anyone you ever wanted to meet to a Roundtable without appearing pushy or obvious. Phyllis, a female friend, longed to get to know Robert, a man she had met at a dining club. Finally, she made it happen by inviting the fellow to a Roundtable. A statuesque and bosomy brunette, Phyllis was CEO of a successful wine business. Her soon-to-be beau accepted her invitation before the words had hardly been spoken, she reported.

Robert, dressed casually in a white turtleneck and slacks, arrived on the dot carrying a pot of Vanda orchids, with a beautiful smile and a gleam in his brown eyes. Both James and Phyllis immersed themselves in the conversation, but it was obvious they longed to be alone together. It must have been love, or lust, at first sight because only a month later they were engaged. They invited all who had witnessed the beginning of this steamy romance to their beach wedding. Did their marriage last? No, but while it did, they gave us a great show, kicking up their heels and flaunting themselves in a way that embarrassed most, but others emulated. Go for it, I say.

CHAPTER THREE

Follow the Fold and Stray No More

Everything is starting to come together nicely! A Party Buddy has been carefully selected along with a delicious yet manageable menu and an eclectic group. Just a few more to-dos's before you start buffing those party shoes. Time and a lack of it (so it seems) is the key reason why get-togethers aren't held outside of birthdays and holidays. You have the same 24 hours as those whom you admire. It can be done. Listen to your wise old teacher. I will help you plan your work so you can work your plan.

Prepare for your party gradually. Trying to do everything in one day will be overwhelming. Savor the planning! Enjoy the journey! Buy and arrange flowers the day before your Roundtable. In major cities you can seriously stretch your dollar using a flower wholesaler.

A timesaving tip; marinate meats and chop vegetables the night before for easy cooking—and to cut back on the odor of garlic and onions in your skin and hair. Keep ingredients in Tupperware containers and when it's cooking time, grab and go!

DANCING ON THE EDGE OF THE WORLD

Opulent table settings with over-the-top themes and five star dining are not only impractical, they are a headache and in bad taste. The focus of a Roundtable is conversation, heart-to-heart and no-holds barred. Keep that in mind.

Let go of any pressure you might feel to make everything

photo perfect. There's no such thing as perfection anyway, so forget about it. You will only stress yourself out and end up looking silly and make your guests uncomfortable. Above all, be REAL. Pretentiousness means pretending so you can impress others. You impress best by being YOURSELF. I'll repeat that. *You impress best by being yourself.* Whatever your background, your education, the amount of money you have or the lack thereof, or your material possessions, so long as you live an honorable life, are reasonably clean and truthful, you are ENOUGH. In our culture we have been swamped with advertising that inculcates us with the idea that our house, car, furniture, clothes have to be just so to be acceptable. Nonsense, baloney, claptrap! If you think material possessions will make you happy it's beyond doubt time to change your attitude, to live your life with integrity and not give a thought to what others may think of you. The important thing is what you think of you. Go into whatever it is with the sure knowledge that you will be successful and that everything is thought up

"Love is in the details"
therefore check, check and double check
that you have what you need before the event:

1. Garnish.
2. Cut lemons and limes.
3. A working wine opener.
4. Kleenex.
5. A charged camera.
6. Proper serving spoons and salad tongs
7. A cleared area for used dishes.
8. Napkins and extra linens should something spill.

You impress best by being yourself.

by someone somewhere at some time or other. Confidence is the name of any game, darlin'. My mom always said, when I was asked to recite a poem in church, "Patsy Lou, speak up, talk to the last row in the church house. Don't be a weak worm of the dust!"

At one of my early Roundtables, I served long-stemmed strawberries with sour cream and brown sugar for dessert. The next day an item in the society pages of the *San Francisco Chronicle* reported "Pat Montandon served long-stemmed strawberries while talking about being on welfare as a child." Well, one would have thought I dropped a bomb in San Francisco Bay, as there was an unholy reaction to that truthful report. My oldest sister, Nina, tried to get a retraction by calling the reporter, who in turn called me. Sadly, Nina considered it shameful to have been on welfare while I considered it to be a blessing in disguise. Nina was eighteen years older than me and I don't like saying it, but she lived an ultraconservative lifestyle. Being so much older than I, she was irritated that I didn't consult with her or invite her to that particular Salon. But, whatever the reason, I have long since forgiven her and didn't dwell on it at the time either. Being on welfare as a child has given me a compassionate view of the world, a view I might not have otherwise had.

SAVING NICE THINGS "FOR GOOD"

Do you have things you're "saving" for special occasions? My grandmother said use the things you consider special. Otherwise you are so busy protecting them, you don't enjoy having whatever it is and in time you end up giving them away. Grandma's bone china or that crystal vase you bought on vacation in Italy—your personal treasures should be shared instead of stored so bring them out; they can act as the impetus for a fantastic story and deeper insight into who you are. *Things* should never define us, but the things we hold dear can say a lot about who we are.

CENTERPIECE—DECORATIN' THE TABLE

When it comes to table décor aim for simple elegance. Arrange flowers cut from your garden in a low vase or cut them right at the bulb base and gently set them in a clear glass bowl of water. Don't stop at flowers, set out collectables, your favorite books, or a family photo, tactile elements that make you, YOU! Remember, *"Everything you need to be happy, you already possess."* Chances are, you have all that you need for a fantastic party and if you don't, well, borrow it.

If a guest is a writer try to have their articles or books on the table. I frequently use them as the centerpiece with perhaps, one rose in a vial laid across a small stack of books. It's very important to have a low centerpiece—whether it's a basket of gleaming apples, jewel-like vegetables, flowers, or a large crystal in a bowl of water.

Whenever I think about table centerpieces, I'm reminded of a dinner party I attended in the Silicon Valley, given by a dot com couple with more money than common sense. Or experience. The showpiece was a magnificent arrangement of white orchids that climbed from the table like a living creature and up to their crystal chandelier. The arrangement could have decorated a mobster's funeral. It was impossible to see anyone else at the table because of that flower tower.

Finally, after bobbing back and forth to talk to a man hidden by the forest of flowers, I could contain myself no longer. My sense of humor got the best of me. I stood up, clinked my glass for quiet, and announced that I would like to propose a toast. "I would like to propose a toast to … to … to The Centerpiece!" I said, causing applause as ripples of laughter reverberated around the table. Then, in the spirit of the moment, each guest reached over and plucked a flower from the centerpiece, bringing the entire edifice down to eye level. Our hostess had the good grace to

> *Remember, "Everything you need to be happy, you already possess."*

On the eve of the Roundtable,
crosscheck the to-do list with your Buddy
and pay special attention to the bathroom.

1. Be sure there is an extra roll of toilet tissue in the bathroom.

2. Fresh liquid soap.

3. Put out a small basket of rolled white terry washcloths to use as hand towels.

4. Be sure used towels and unappealing things of that sort of are out of sight.

5. Make the mirrors shine!

6. A flower in a bud vase or a lit candle is a nice inexpensive touch.

laugh. Later, she thanked me and said she had no idea how to set a table, but she learned. Simple is always better. We were gathered there to see each other, to converse, not to admire an overpriced bunch of flowers.

SETTING THE MOOD

You have made sure your guests will be taken care of; now allow extra time for the host—you—so that you feel pretty and self-confident come party time. When you look relaxed, others, who might be nervous, will relax as well. When you look your best, you're twice as glad to see other people. Take a deep breath, in through the nose, out through the mouth. Repeat five times. Better? I thought so. This will be a fantastic experience, the start of many, and here is where we begin.

Some folks will be in your home for the first time, so think about that old adage, "You have only one chance to make a first

Don't even think about a drink of anything alcoholic! A tipsy host is just that, tipsy and silly.

impression." Disheveled hair and a red sweaty face doesn't say welcome in the same way a put-together outfit and sincere smile does! If you have help today, use it. If you're feeling nervous, then light a scented candle and play your favorite music. Music, as we know, sooths the savage beast and creates a relaxing environment. Soon your jitters will fall away. Is your stomach still jumping? Don't even think about a drink of anything alcoholic! A tipsy host is just that, tipsy and silly. A better suggestion is for you to step outside, close your eyes and feel the warm sun on your face, or if you live in the Arctic, feel the wind and snow on your face and be grateful. Think of ten things for which you are thankful. I guarantee you will be so happy when you open your eyes that your nerves will be settled and the sense of gratitude you experienced will flow from you to your guests. If you have time to walk around the block or knock out a yoga pose or two, do it. Be sure no one catches you with your butt to the sun in a downward dog pose or they will really wonder what kind of party this is.

INCOMING!

The doorbell chimes and your stomach gives birth to butterflies. In all your planning, did you forget about the living beings that would be joining you? If this is your first Roundtable or your fiftieth, everyone gets antsy at this moment. You're only nervous because you're excited and you're excited because you've done a fantastic job! One last deep breathe. Open the door. Here we go.

Warm welcomes don't mean a loud, shrill "Hiiii!" It is the heart behind the hello that counts. Give a special greeting to each person; a kind smile, genuine embrace or a firm handshake, and your guests will know you are authentically glad to see them rather than being focused on the boiling pots or your tight new shoes. I suggest the heartfelt royal-welcome; "Am I ever glad to see you!" Instantly, your guests will be glad they came.

Greet each person by name and introduce early arrivals to each other. Remembering names can be tricky, some days I forget my own. If you are terrible with names (like I am) ask your Buddy to quiz you ahead of time. She gives you the first name, and you give the last. Close your eyes, visualize the person, describe their hair, stature and think of two points from their bio that stood out for you. Then quiz your Buddy. If the excitement causes you to have a brain fart and forget the name of a friend, laugh it off! Try saying, "I talk to this woman four times a day and can't remember her name!" It happens and people understand.

If you have a guest of honor, be sure to stand near the entry with him or her, introducing each new arrival at the beginning of the party. After a reasonable time you and your honored guest may circulate, but you are responsible throughout for the comfort and pleasure of the guest who is your party's raison d'être.

Once the bulk of your guests have arrived, station yourself near the front door and let people mingle. The repetition of "this is so and so, this is so and so" interrupts and annoys. Step aside and let the connections spark naturally while introducing new arrivals to a few people. Always have a place cleared for coats or outdoor shoes. A ten-pack of hangers can be picked up at a dollar store, but an empty bed will do fine. If your husband is sleeping there, just cover him up, laugh and close the door.

TO THE TABLE NOW

While your company chats over friendly small talk, lead people over to a tray of juice or wine. A full bar is overkill for a luncheon. I once took advantage of a champagne brunch and had a glass of bubbly with every course. By 3 P.M. I had a splitting headache and my afternoon was ruined. Cocktails may loosen tongues, but you don't want to be responsible for belligerent tirades or a mid-day hangover. Pitchers of lemonade, ice tea, or sparkling water with limes along with a bottle of wine are all you need. Be sure to have non-alcoholic choices for those who choose not to drink, extra ice, and proper glassware. Once everyone has had a sip and a chat, lead them to the table.

As we mentioned earlier, plan your seating well ahead of time, splitting up regular friends. Think back to the bios everyone sent in. Mix it up! Place cards, with the name written on the front and back for all at the table to see, are a thoughtful detail. They look lovely and we can all appreciate assistance when there are 10 names to remember. That planning avoids the awkward stammering of trying to seat ten adults at once, "Charles you sit next to Amanda, no wait, I want you beside me, no, that won't work." I

Place cards, with the name written on the front and back for all at the table to see, are a thoughtful detail.

can see eyes rolling now. Hungry people aimlessly milling around the table distracts from the flow of your salon and gets it off to a rough start. Again, the goal is for people to meet one another. If they choose their own seats, you can be sure they will cozy up next to an old friend before they engage a stranger. Planning this important step takes only a few moments, yet it sets the tone for the entire afternoon.

Being welcoming and friendly is important. No need to zip around the room fussing over everyone, just keep your eyes open and quietly communicate with your Buddy and any other helpers. Again, this is why you have help—you host, they serve. Have a system in place before hand, perhaps at your test dinner, and have your Buddy look for the following; check wine and water glasses for refills. Are there knives for the butter? There should be a serving utensil for each dish and be sure that your lovely table setting isn't covered in crumpled napkins, dirty plates or a load of empty glasses. Listen for a break in the conversation as well. Smooth, seamless, and invisible is how servers should operate.

Too much food on a plate dampens ones appetite. It's true that less is more.

I attended a lunch not long ago where the sous-chef took it upon herself to 1) wear a cocktail dress to work and 2) greet guests at the door (some folks thought SHE was the host!). During a tense confession in the luncheon conversation, this charming but dense woman interrupted a guest, only to excessively gush her appreciation and share her weight loss story. Uh, say what now? I think she was expecting applause! Rule number one, the focus is on the guests, so please stress that point. Service industry professionals have a sixth sense to be invisible while cleaning and clearing.

When all your guests are seated you'll want to serve the first course. If someone is late, continue with lunch despite their tardiness. You may instinctively feel that it is rude to serve your meal before all are in attendance, but it is unfair to the other guests to hold up lunch. When folks are looking at their watch or the door, it distracts everyone. Since you are in charge of the conversation as well as food, you will want to remain seated while serving. With the entrees on a serving table, allow your Party Buddy to assist with filling the plates and taking them to the other guests. Please do not overfill the plates. Too much food on a plate dampens ones appetite. It's true that less is more.

Don't overwhelm yourself; and do ask for help if you need it. Juggle too many balls and you'll drop one. If you can afford a hired chef and server for the afternoon, well, hooray. Otherwise put that Party Buddy to good use and/or ask another guest to give you a hand. Again, conversation is the focus. Serve and clear the table efficiently so conversation can continue to flow smoothly.

Don't overwhelm yourself; and do ask for help if you need it.

WRANGLING HELP ON A BUDGET

- Ask your favorite server from a local restaurant (well in advance) if he or she would like to earn additional money at a private lunch. Budget for their time before asking. Be sure to include an amount for a tip.
- Hire a few well-mannered teenagers to do the cleanup. Tell them to not clean up the table in front of your guests. Clanging dishes are distracting for everyone. Just quietly remove plates one at a time, and place them in the kitchen.
- Or set up a sideboard so guests can serve themselves before seating. Borrow or rent chafing dishes for hot food and extra utensils if you don't own such items.

DANGER AHEAD

If one of your new friends starts to show the telltale signs of, well, getting drunk, let your Buddy know to go slow on the drinks—extra ice and hold back on refilling their wine glass. Differing opinions are embraced of course, but if the Tea Party member and the Greenpeace spokesman are close to trading blows or schoolyard insults, let it happen. This is not your grandma's kind of luncheon. Get all your guests involved in this brew! You are the host—you hold the power! Your guests are there to forge new friendships and scrap it out in the driveway if necessary.

While some shout for attention, others become introverts when in a social setting so give a special introduction to an individual that may hesitate to speak up. One such guest at a Roundtable many years ago was renowned folk singer, Malvina Reynolds. Malvina had brought her guitar. She stood up from the table and said, "I'm not much of a talker but I'll sing one of my songs for you." With that, she sang *Little Boxes*, her billboard topping composition as well as several of her new songs. It was a delightful interlude and gave us all a lift of spirit.

Finally, there are six important DO'S & DON'TS:

1. Less Is More

Regardless of advertisements trying to make us feel less than we are unless we buy their product, less really is more. Really. The size of your home doesn't matter nor does your furniture, but it should be open and clutter free. People shouldn't feel like they are running a gauntlet in a kid's playroom, stepping over toys and other debris. Breakables and knickknacks can be tucked away safely in a bedroom or spare closet. Today you're collecting memories, not things.

2. Eat and Let Live

Some cultures express love through food. The more you eat, the more you love! I can hear my Russian friends now, "Eat, Patricciaa, only dogs like bones!" Sorry Alevitina, but pressuring guests to gorge isn't hospitable. Others might take you up on your offer and drink like it's their last night before jail and then you have another issue with which to cope. The Roundtable Salons focus on heart-to-heart conversation, being vulnerable and expressing true feelings and opinions. When you aren't all there, you can't give your all. Keep the tequila on ice for another occasion.

3. Send in the Clowns

As the host and mediator, guests will automatically defer to you to direct the conversation. If you are making googly-eyes with a handsome stranger, or giving a snarky commentary to your neighbor, you can't actively guide the talk and guests will feel like they need to vie for your attention to be heard. Make sure to involve everyone in the conversation. It's fun.

4. You'll Never Get away from Me

Martyrdom as a spectator sport went out several centuries ago.

Nattering on about how much trouble this event was, how you drove all over town ... honey, save the recap for tomorrow over coffee. You would rather be praised for skill than for effort, anyway. Skill always appears effortless; a wonderful host leaves her guests wondering, "How does she do it?" rather than droning on and on about it. Like a good server, your function as the hostess is to create the fantasy that guests are being fully catered to. The food magically appears hot and delicious. Dishes are whisked away and not another thought is given to them.

Schlepping about the dining room with gravy on your blouse and a fistful of crusty forks takes the glamour down about eight notches. Side note: Never, never rise and scrap and slop around with the dishes in front of guests. Remove used dishes from the table, stack them in the kitchen and walk away. If someone offers to help, dismiss it by saying, "Oh no, my butler will take care of them." Smile and change the subject.

5. It's Too Late to Apologize

The key to being a great host and a great anything is confidence. If there are details that have been overlooked, who cares? Unless the food is in flames these are minor hiccups, and even then you can always order in. In most performances only the entertainer notices the mistakes. Allow your guests to enjoy this show! Apologizing profusely makes you shrink down and makes everyone else uncomfortable. If you are complimented on your party, or on the dress you are wearing by all means reply graciously. Don't say, "Well, I do the best I can in this tiny place of mine" or "That old thing? Heavens, I've had it for years! " If you do you are belittling the judgment of the person who was kind enough to offer you a compliment. You put him or her in a position where he must insist, and go on at length about something that ought to have been passed off lightly. It's much better to say, "I'm glad you like it" or "How good of you to tell me." Then everyone is happy.

The last tip is an extra bit of giving, the extra bit of loving care that counts in life. Create an atmosphere around you which is yours alone in the arrangements you've made, the people you've chosen, the care with which you've studied each detail of your party, and the sense of warmth and gaiety you communicate to your guests. Put your heart into it, and your luncheon will be something no one else could have given.

Part of your career as a topnotch Roundtable hostess will depend on your skill as a guest. So, what kind of a guest are you? Do you drop by unannounced, let yourself in, and head straight for the fridge? Unless you're twelve years old, I certainly hope not! Even then, you can be quickly trained to do better.

Let's assume that you know the basic rules; don't chug your wine, or pick at the food, don't swear in front of the children, and please refrain from making passes at husbands and college-age sons. I know Cougars are all the rage, but really, don't. Always say, "Thank you very much. I had a very nice time." Most of us are taught these little refinements at an early age, and yet there are a good many important matters about being a good guest that are all too often forgotten or ignored.

6. RSVP Please

As a hostess, you will soon know how important this initial step is. Virtually every decision hinges on how many people are attending the Roundtable. Think it, do it. When you get the invitation, check your calendar and reply at your earliest convenience, ideally within 24 hours. If you can attend, perfect, your seat will be saved, if you cannot make it, or you are unsure, still reply promptly, and explain the situation. The host will appreciate it and she might suggest you "drop by at the last moment, if possible", but give her the option to decide and plan for that. This is a standard rule for any party, but as you are learning, the Roundtable requires some group participation before the actual lunch itself.

YOU'RE NO LONGER A STRANGER TO ME

For the Roundtable, it is not customary to bring a guest. Leave it up to the host to decide how the group dynamics should work. Do not ask to bring anyone, unless the circumstances are very unusual. If you aren't sure, ask the host, and I said ask, not guilt trip and badger. If you get a thumbs-up, encourage your guest to write their bio and respond to the host, thanking her in advance.

PLAY A SIMPLE MELODY

Use your judgment and consult your host if there is any doubt in your mind about what would be appropriate to wear. A Sunday lunch in someone's home means business casual. Not stiff work clothes, or liquid leggings, but think of what you'd wear on an afternoon with a family member. Men: a collared shirt. Women: A touchable texture in your most flattering color. Your host hasn't knocked herself out preparing for this lunch just to have you arrive looking as if you pulled your clothes out from between the mattress! It's just plain thoughtless and insulting! You owe it to your host, as well as yourself, to look fresh and lovely for this special afternoon.

A GIFT FOR THE HOST

Flowers are a thoughtful gesture, but if each guest arrives with a bouquet, your poor host will be scrambling for a vase and your arrangement might end up in a kid's plastic cup! If this is the first time to be in your host's home, a bottle of wine, a small potted plant, or sweet treats are all nice gestures, as are candles. If you are the guest of honor, and want to offer a substantial thank you in flowers, telephone your hostess ahead of time. Ask her what colors would be suitable, and have your flowers delivered the day before the party.

ANOTHER OPENING, ANOTHER SHOW

Notice and study your surroundings so that you can compliment your host. Has she made special arrangements for the party or changed the décor since your last visit? You'd look a bit daft if you hadn't noticed the fresh coat of bright yellow paint on the walls or the new furniture. Turn those senses on! The scents (Lunch smells divine), sights, (What great light in this room! Is that original crown molding?), and sounds (Oh I just love Sade's new album, are you seeing her when she comes to town?). Tell her she looks great—can't go wrong there. So many people go through the motions at parties, dishing out halfhearted hellos, minimal interaction with others, eat, drink, and exit. Jeez, come by when you can't stay so long. Not everyone has the help you do when throwing an event, but when it's done right, say something.

THANKS FOR THE MEMORIES

Obviously do this before you leave, but a nicely worded little note shows your sincerity. There isn't a better way to spend forty-seven cents and a few minutes of your time. It's a formal practice that suggests extra care and effort. However it is perfectly okay to call you host afterward, up to two days after the event. If you have followed all these tips and didn't break grandma's heirloom china, you'll probably be invited back.

Not so fast guests, there are a few more Don'ts to consider.

I'M LATE, I'M LATE, FOR A VERY IMPORTANT DATE

"The surest way to be late is to have plenty of time." It isn't nice, and it isn't fashionable either. It implies that you had more important things to do than to come on time or relatively so. If you suffer from chronic lateness, don't shrug it off; impress your host by being the first to arrive, but don't arrive too early. For Roundtable purposes, you want to be there for the initial mingling with guests and to join the conversation from the start. If you have to leave early, you should have explained the circumstances to your hostess when you accepted her invitation. When you leave a party early, slip out quietly so as not to distract the other guests, and make your farewells ahead of time or as unobtrusive as possible.

WALL FLOWER

Get off the wall, wallflower, and get in the game! No one is asking you to put on a pink feather boa and start a Soul Train line, but arrive with a positive, enthusiastic attitude! Be glad to meet people, shake hands firmly (the limp drip handshake is THE worst) and share some interesting tidbits of conversation. You have everyone's bios, so when reading them ahead of time, think of a question for that person. Communication is what this party is all about, so communicate. If small talk isn't your forte, try walking up to someone-smile and introduce yourself. You were asked to be here because this fabulous host finds you truly interesting. Shake that doubt off, you deserve to be here and have been looking forward to this for a near month! The best thing you can do is act like it!

IT'S MY PARTY, I CAN CRY IF I WANT TO

There are other people to consider as well as you. This isn't time to test out your comedy material either. Folks came for a Roundtable, not the YOU show. An anecdote or two are plenty and if you can't help being in the spotlight, by all means hire a hall and sell tickets.

YOU CAN SHINE, BEST DO IT BEHIND ME

Do speak your mind and your truth. Grilling others with personal questions, yet refusing to answer any yourself is not Roundtable etiquette. As well as saying nothing, interrupting, instigating, and annoying your hostess or other guests. The invitation explained what the rules of the Roundtable are so don't act surprised now. It's up to you to realize what this tone is and cooperate.

HONEY, PLEASE

One gloomy guest can douse the spirit of an entire party, so if you're having a Debbie Downer day, notify your host, stay home, and have a hot bath. Faking your interest exhausts you and everyone else. Your host can't fix all your problems. She has nine others to consider. What do you want her to do when you're knocking at the door, hum glum and start rattling on about your bad day and horrible life? Brush your hair and rub your back? Don't be upset when she asks you to come by another time when you're feeling better. Your hostess is counting on you to help make things interesting and pleasant. If you aren't up for it, pass.

HELPFUL HARRIETT

We don't want to confuse you now, helpful and cooperating are two different things. Cooperating means going with the flow. Helpful Harriet insists on running out to the kitchen, and banging things all around, just when you had yourself and the other guests half convinced that Jeeves was in charge of everything. Don't pull a Harriet. Helpful Harriet leaps to her feet in the midst of the most delightful conversation, and shrieks, "Do let me help you clear these dishes, please; you have so much to do," and that's where H.H. gives herself away. If she really wanted to be helpful, she would have asked you quietly ahead of time, "Would you like me to be in charge of clearing the table, or bringing in the coffee, perhaps?" And she would have taken a simple no for an answer. What Helpful Harriet wants, obviously, is attention and appreciation. Not having any clear sense of herself, she seeks approval by performing domestic chores as conspicuously as possible. No, no, *no*.

CHAPTER FOUR

I Am Woman

When the idea of creating a Roundtable Salon popped into my mind, I was slightly nervous at the thought of bringing strangers together for deep conversations. Was I up to the job? I wasn't afraid of entertaining—I had done a lot of that through the years and I enjoyed it. But I wanted the Roundtable to be more substantial than a casual dinner party. I shared my dream with Merla Zellerbach, whom I had known for years. She has a gentle air about her and is a loyal friend. I knew I would need her support to make my fantasy a reality.

"Look at it this way, Pat," she said, "Your guests won't be strangers once they are seated at your table. Then you can just be yourself and treat them like old friends. I'm looking forward to this." Her enthusiasm helped me overcome my concerns.

My first Roundtables were for women only. It was 1976 and the height of the women's movement. However, I didn't know any feminists. I had only seen them on television or read about them in the newspaper. At that time, being a feminist was controversial. I didn't want to burn my bra, personally, but in my heart I was cheering those women on.

The most prominent feminist in the San Francisco Bay Area was Aileen Hernandez, who had succeeded Betty Friedan as president of the National Organization for Women and was largely responsible for its phenomenal growth and influence. She was a dynamic leader, nationally known, and much in demand as speaker and consultant all over the country. If I invited her, would she turn me down? I did, and she did. Then I invited her again and she accepted. She became a Roundtable regular and one of its biggest boosters.

Years later, she told guests at my table how she felt when she received my first invitation. "I had read that Pat was a socialite, and I thought 'What could I possibly have in common with that woman and her rich friends?' But when the second invitation came, my curiosity got the better of me. I came to the Roundtable, and I've been returning ever since, just like a bad penny."

In that instance, courage and persistence paid off. Aileen became a valued friend. Through her, I've met the top leaders in the women's movement: Betty Friedan, Gloria Steinem, Del Martin, Phyllis Lyon, and many more. All have come to Roundtables. They still come, although the luncheons have long since changed to include men. Inevitably, some of the men have been male chauvinists, which makes for lively debates—although, that mindset has changed since the 70's, *thank Goddess.*

Among the first men I invited was a sophisticated and successful entrepreneur. He had funded the construction of numerous structures and entire towns. He was a Big Time Guy, well known—and at a loss for words at my table. He was unaccustomed to speaking from the heart; everything was a sales pitch. He was bewildered. When I asked him The Question—"Other than family members, whom do you remember as being the most kind to you as a child?" He slapped his napkin on the table and announced, "I have no idea what you folks are talking about. We all know that wives were created to take care of the home and babies, not sit and

If I invited her, would she turn me down?
I did, and she did. Then I invited her
again and she accepted.
She became a Roundtable regular and one
of its biggest boosters.

talk about women's rights. Men supply the money that powers the home and allows the little woman (he actually said that) to buy jewelry and stuff." The entire table was clamoring to talk, but Mr. Big Bucks was out the door, off to buy a good cigar and have a whiskey with "decent folks," he said. I am happy to report that there were plenty of men who disagreed with him that day and they still attend these luncheons.

But back to how it all began: a friend and I were having coffee, discussing whom we'd like to talk to and about what. This is probably the best way to begin, for anyone contemplating a Roundtable of their own. Involve a friend or two and they'll think of interesting people you can invite.

Two things can go wrong when you're making a guest list. Either you can't think of anybody interesting to invite or you invite too many. Let's deal with the first possibility. You decide that there aren't enough fascinating people in town to populate one luncheon, let alone several. But have faith. Once you reach out to strangers, you'll learn that everyone has a gripping story. Some of them will shake up your world in a way that will invigorate you for the rest of your life.

Consider inviting the editor of a local newspaper or a reporter. They know what's happening in and around town and who is making it happen. Their livelihoods depend on this. You might consult the news as well to find out who has just returned from an exciting trip or who might be entertaining visitors from another town, city, or country.

Are people obsessing over inflation? Why not invite an economics teacher, a banker, or a knowledgeable person who can answer your questions about the economy? Worried that your children aren't learning basics in school? Invite the president of the school board, an elementary teacher or principal, and somebody from the PTA. If you have strong feelings about a topic, remember not to speechify, but to participate—to listen and learn as well as opine.

Consider the local eccentric when making up your guest list. Every community has one or two, and you might be surprised at the color they add to your gathering. You and all your guests will have an unusual experience and learn how others live and think, which will give you insights you might not otherwise have. If it doesn't work out, so what? Try someone else next time.

In the 70's, we wanted to meet women with careers that were previously reserved for men—female doctors, lawyers, and truck drivers, for instance. We also wanted to meet men doing work traditionally associated with women, such as a male nurse, secretary, or househusband. Don't forget to include guests from other races, religions, and ethnic groups. They can offer new perspectives on everything from the state of the world to religion, holidays, and how minorities fare in your community. Don't be afraid to invite people with differing viewpoints. If everybody around your table is just alike, outside and inside, your luncheon is in danger of being dull, dull, *dull* and you will learn nothing.

A celebrity now and then adds glamour and sparkle to a Roundtable gathering. So don't hesitate to invite celebrities if they're coming to town to conduct the local symphony, autograph books, talk to the Rotary Club, or star in a theatre group. Check the local theatre and club listing to see who is expected.

The person or group responsible for bringing the celebrity to town can usually tell you how they to reach them. If it's someone who writes a column for the newspaper or whose interview appeared in the media, you could send the invitation in care of the newspaper, radio, or television station. Social media is also a great way to contact people. When Hermione Gingold came to San Francisco to perform in a play, I invited her to lunch by calling the theater and asking where I could send her invitation. Once she sat at the Roundtable and realized this wasn't your typical luncheon,

Consider the local eccentric when making up your guest list.

she exclaimed, "Oh God! We are actually going to talk!"

Don't be timid about issuing your invitation just because you fear that a well-known person may turn you down. You've a 50/50 chance that he or she will accept. Celebrities have to eat, after all. Why not with you? They frequently have unscheduled time and, like anyone else, they get lonely in strange towns. By sending Roundtable invitations to celebrities I didn't know, I've met a number of inspiring people from Steve Martin, Werner Erhard, Beverly Sills, Harvey Milk, Betty Freidan, Daniel Ellsburg, and well – the list goes on and on. I discovered that most people in the Arts make great guests. They are open, friendly, and man, can they tell a story.

YOUR GUEST LIST

Now, let's consider the second mistake you might make in putting together your guest list, which is inviting too many people. You think of three, and your friend thinks of two, then each of you thinks of several more. Before you know it, you have fifteen or twenty. That's way too many! Save some of them for another time. Ten is the maximum number you should consider for one sitting. Less if your table won't accommodate them easily. People can't concentrate on what's being said if they have to worry about getting jabbed in the ribs by a neighbor's elbow or spilling soup in their lap. Also, with more than ten, the conversation has a tendency to turn into speech making by the articulate and silent listening by the less assured. You want spontaneous give and take. That's more easily accomplished among a smaller number of guests.

Think about the size of your table and how many chairs you have before you send out invitations. Think about your table shape, too. Of course, you can have a Roundtable without a round table, but I advise against it. Conversation at a rectangular table can fall flatter than an underdone soufflé! You can talk to the person on your right and your left and immediately across the table— but that's it. Often you can't even see some of those with whom you are supposed to be dining.

A case in point was what I refer to as The Overwhelming Flagship. A round-shaped table gives everyone a view of those at the table and a chance to interact with everyone. When someone speaks, all other diners can see and hear the speaker and respond to body language as well to their voice. The company is less apt to split into small groups, each discussing a separate topic, and the hostess will find it easier to direct the talk and see that everyone has an opportunity to participate.

Your table isn't round? Don't despair. You can invest in an inexpensive, round, plywood table top, preferably hinged in the middle for easy storage. Place it on the table you have or on a regular restaurant base.

A Roundtable doesn't have to be a luncheon, either. A Saturday or Sunday brunch might work better in your community. Or you might try evening suppers. These usually demand that you invite married people as couples, but do include singles too. Don't try to pattern your dinner after Noah's Ark though; your guests aren't there to mate so it's perfectly fine to have more men than women or vice versa. Once you have decided on a date, a guest list, and how many you can comfortably accommodate, you are ready to send out invitations. Please, no "What Where When" cards or the kind with pre-printed flower sprigs, and definitely do not use notepaper with gaudy patterns or happy faces. You want your guests to know that the Roundtable is no ordinary affair. Your event is well thought out, carefully planned, and each guest is special. Your invitations should convey this message.

Because I give Roundtables frequently, I have my invitations engraved with blank spaces for the guest's name and the date. If

Please, no "What Where When" cards or the kind with pre-printed flower sprigs, and definitely do not use notepaper with gaudy patterns or happy faces.

you want to try out the idea of a Roundtable before you invest in printed invitations, write your invitations in longhand on good, heavy paper. However, with all the options offered online, the days of buying stamps and having engraved invitations seem to have gone the way of the lava lamp. Email invitations work well and elicit quick responses. But if you really want to make a good impression, consider going backwards to the good old days of rules and manners! Shock your guests with actual cursive writing! A written invitation is sure to get a lot more attention than an Internet missive. In any case this is the format I use whether online or on the back of a dove:

Pat Montandon

And Members of the Roundtable

Request

The Honor of Your Presence

At a Roundtable Luncheon

Twelve-thirty

Sunday, October 25, 20XX

Green Street (street parking available)

San Francisco, California 40825

R.S.V.P. By October 20, 20XX

via pmontandon@aol.com or 310-859-1246

Dress: Sunday Casual

(please include a short bio in your reply)

I include the guest's name, the luncheon date, my telephone number and a deadline to respond, usually one week before the event. That way I give myself enough time to invite someone else should an invitee not be able to attend. You might also want to add the time the luncheon will be over. For example, "until 2 p.m." This is a courtesy to those guests who may need to catch a plane or a train, or let the babysitter know what time they'll return.

If you and your spouse are giving the Roundtable together, issue the invitations in both your names "Mary Smith and John Jones," or "Mary and John Jones." Don't use "Mr. And Mrs. John Jones." If you do, the strangers you've invited will call you "Mrs. Jones" (they can't call both you and your husband "John") while your friends are calling you Mary, and that's guaranteed to keep those who don't know you feeling that they're outsiders who haven't been invited into the inner circle.

Send invitations three to four weeks in advance so as to allow busy people time to schedule your event into their calendars. If your handwriting is illegible, and you hate to lick stamps but love the talk on the telephone, you might do away with written invitations and call the people you want to invite.

I frequently follow up a written invitation with a telephone call, particularly to guests who haven't been to a Roundtable before.

There are advantages to inviting a person over the phone. You make direct contact with prospective guests so that neither of you feels a stranger when you meet at the luncheon. You can answer questions about parking, and what to wear. You're alerted if there are foods this guest can't eat, and you'll know at once whether or not this person will accept your invitation, so that you can quickly invite someone else if need be.

I frequently follow up a written invitation with a telephone call, particularly to guests who haven't been to a Roundtable before. Often, after the guest list is complete, I send it to all guests, along with a short bio for each person. Glancing it over, guests can anticipate conversation topics. I've found this adds a degree of comfort when everyone gets together. They have thought about what they want to ask or tell other guests with particular interests. Sometimes they even bring newspaper clippings or a book to share.

My note, sent a week before the Roundtable, is handwritten and goes something like this: "Looking forward to seeing you at the Roundtable on June 22. Thought you might like to know something about others who will be there." For example:

Joe Flynn • Author of three books on meditation

Marry Smith • Homemaker interested in Modern Art

Tom Mallory • Former convict; founder of a rehabilitation program for ex-cons

Jane Doe • Gray Panther Party, concerned with welfare for the aged

Mimi La Fou • Formerly a topless dancer, now a law clerk

Once you've done this, the preliminaries are over. You can start preparing for the actual event. Are you concerned that your plywood round table is an eyesore? That's easily remedied. I've made skirts to the floor to cover mine. Linen or polyester are easy to work with and don't require much care. Brightly patterned or flowered bed sheets make attractive table coverings and have the advantage of being permanent press; meaning they don't need to be ironed. You can make napkins out of the sheet material, too. I frequently cover the basic cloth with tablecloths of varying lengths and designs. Make it gala. And don't mind that you've never seen it done your way before. The Roundtable isn't typical—why should your table be?

Plan menus to be unobtrusive. At a Roundtable you're featuring conversation. Everything else takes second place. That means that you, as the host, must be most concerned with the talk, not with the food. If you can hire somebody to cook and serve, do so.

If not, enlist children and friends, crock-pots and microwaves, toaster ovens and heated serving trays.

The object is to keep you seated, not hopping up and down during the meal. You might serve a hot soup. Let a friend bring it to the table. Followed by a cold entree, which you serve from a serving table beside you. Followed by dessert and coffee, waiting at the buffet. Or you might have a cold soup and an entree waiting in the crock-pot or even at your side on a serving table. There are any number of dishes and menus that don't impinge on conversation or keep a hostess dashing back and forth to the kitchen. But the logistics should be carefully worked out beforehand. Don't try to do something elaborate. Baked Alaska is out. You want the conversation to star, not the food.

SEATING

Forget the advice of seating a table by alternating sexes. There's no law that says a man can't be seated next to a man, or a woman next to a woman. As far as possible, try to mix talkers and listeners. Mix your friends and Roundtable regulars with newcomers. Above all, if you insist on inviting married couples, separate them! You want them to participate as individuals, not as halves of a whole. If you have a celebrity guest, he or she should be seated on your right.

By all means make place cards. Put the full name Dr. Mary Burns on one side and Mary on the other. The "Mary" side faces the diner and tells her where to sit. The side with the full name faces outward so that other guests can identify her. Then no one has to apologize for not remembering a name or remain silent because he or she isn't sure how to address the person with whom he wishes to speak. Place cards are a big help to the hostess, too, who has a lot on her mind besides remembering names.

I find it enormously helpful to keep a list of guests next to me on the table, with notations about their expertise or interests.

If your Roundtable is in the evening, you'll want to give special attention to lighting. Lights that are ideal for reading can be too harsh for an intimate gathering. They make everybody look austere and forbidding. Invest in pink light bulbs for your lamps and lots of candles for your table. Harsh lighting inhibits conversation. Soft, subtle lighting puts people in the mood to reveal themselves to others. Besides, everyone looks better by candlelight.

You'll probably select your centerpiece last because you assume it will be flowers. Flowers are always beautiful in the center of the table, but if they are too tall, they can impede conversation. If you must have long-stemmed roses, be sure they aren't at eye level and arrange them in small, slender groups in small vases placed strategically about the table.

I personally like low centerpieces, and I don't always use flowers. Sometimes I use attractive weeds. Remember that all flowers are, in truth, cultivated weeds. Heaping baskets of vegetables are attractive, too. Occasionally the containers should be the eye-catcher. Seashells for instance—you can put anything in them, such as a small plant, after dinner candies, or small rocks. Your guests will remember the shells. On a hot day I once used a large clear crystal in the center of a scalloped edged bowl with ice cubes surrounding it! It was simple but elegant.

If this were a fairy tale, I would tell you now that your careful planning will guarantee that nothing will go wrong on the day of the Roundtable. I must report honestly that despite careful planning, small and large things have gone wrong for me and will again, I'm sure.

Some guests have difficult names and though you practice saying them, you'll sometimes mispronounce them. I have. I've even mistaken one guest for another. At one event, I was expecting two dark-haired women, neither of whom I had met before, Marcia Brandwynne, TV anchorwoman, and Joan Baez, the folk singer. When Marcia arrived, I greeted and introduced her as Joan. We still laugh about it. She's since become a good friend and a Roundtable regular. She frequently walks in, announcing, "I am not Joan Baez."

Once, I hired a highly recommended chef to cook for a luncheon whose guests included some well-known foodies. I wanted to impress them—and I'm sure they'll remember it. The chef didn't show and at the last minute, I sent out for Kentucky Fried Chicken. We put the buckets of chicken on the table and dug in. It was like a picnic! There was lots of laughter and the foodies ate as much as anybody.

At another Roundtable, three guests failed to appear. You can remove a place from a set table. Even two. But when you take away three places, you are left with awkward gaps. So I asked the cook and the two women who were serving to join in. They did, and we talked about what it's like to work in someone else's home, the pay scale, the injustices, and the pluses. Since then, these women—Lee Weinhold, Idessa Hopper, and Helen Zurcher—have been very much a part of the Roundtable alumni. What I'm trying to tell you with these reminiscences is that nothing that happens is a total disaster unless you allow it to be. Chances are that, with careful planning, everything will go off without a hitch. But if the worst happens, don't panic. You can deal with anything if you have the right attitude.

In deciding to put together a Roundtable, you've embarked on an incredible adventure. You're not trying to prove that you are a flawless hostess or the world's greatest cook. You're just bringing interesting people together for mutually satisfying conversation. Your sole concern should be that nothing interferes with this objective, even if your guests eat peanut butter sandwiches that they put together themselves. If, in the meantime, they get acquainted, exchange ideas, and are nourished in mind and spirit, you can count your Roundtable a success.

The chef didn't show and at the last minute, I sent out for Kentucky Fried Chicken.

You may give dozens of Roundtable Salons and never have to cope with calamities. I hope you do. But I can also tell

As you look over your table, waiting for guests to arrive, you are embarking on a journey you will always remember. you from my years of hosting Roundtables, that the ones I remember most fondly and that are most dotingly dredged up by Roundtable alumni are those at which the unexpected happened. Nothing brings people more closely together than an emergency. Keeping this in mind, you should be able to muster confidence that your Roundtable will be a triumph, no matter what happens. And it will be.

The day of the Roundtable dawns, and you are ready. The table is set, the place cards in place, and the food ready for easy, unobtrusive serving. You have also done homework about your guests, reading what they've written or what has been written about them, perhaps talking to friends who know them. You've made a list with key words about each guest, which you'll refer to throughout the afternoon. Something like this, perhaps:

Dr. John (Jack) Jones • Surgeon; hobby is needlepoint

Maxine Smith • Teacher specializing in remedial reading; raises bonsai

Doris Brown • Writes children's books, also poetry

As you look over your table, waiting for guests to arrive, you are embarking on a journey you will always remember. Now is the time to put on background music, something soft, slow, and soothing. It will help both you and your guests relax. But please turn it off after the first few guests have arrived.

It's now time to talk!

CHAPTER FIVE

Well, Hello Dolly

Greet each guest warmly, by name, and tell each one how glad you are that he or she has come. (Don't forget to direct them to the phone dock! We're here to talk, not text.) If you have someone helping, that person can take the guest's drink order after the guest is seated. If you are doing the serving yourself, you may want to lead guests to the sideboard on which there is a decanter of white wine, or a pitcher of fruit juice, or a pitcher of sparking water. It isn't necessary to have a complete bar set up, but it does help break the ice to offer your guests a beverage when they arrive.

If yours is a household in which alcoholic beverages aren't usually served, you needn't make an exception in this case. In fact I rarely serve more than wine or champagne and, of course, water at my luncheons. The idea isn't to drink together, but to talk together. It's true, a little alcohol can loosen tongues, but too much can addle brains, and that doesn't make for stimulating conversation.

I like to seat my guests at the table as soon as they arrive. In that way, conversation can begin at once and doesn't have to be interrupted with a general move to the table and a search for designated places. Introduce each new person quickly to the others at the table and tell the newcomer briefly what is being discussed. "We were just talking about the graying of society, and Jane was telling us that she doesn't think that means we'll necessarily become a more conservative nation. Why not, Jane?"

This puts the conversation back on track and gives the group a chance to finish the topic it was exploring. However, if the conversation wasn't going anywhere when the newcomer arrived, it's a good opportunity to give it a new direction. After introducing the latest guest, you might, for instance, explain that he is putting together a rehabilitation program for exconvicts in the community and ask him to tell about it.

Invite guests to participate in each topic. Encourage them to interrupt the speaker so that ideas flow and don't become speechifying. Go for it darlin'—a host should be prepared to back guests up and make all remarks seamless and natural.

When all the guests have arrived and are seated, you'll want to serve the first course. I've even done this before all the guests arrived if one or two were extremely late. It's unfair to the other guests to hold up lunch until it makes them late getting back to the office or other afternoon commitments. Since you are in charge of conversation as well food, you'll probably want to remain seated while serving. If you haven't hired help, fill the plates from the serving table beside you and let a friend or two get up from the table and take the plates to the other guests.

The serving of different courses can punctuate the conversation, bringing one topic to an end and giving you a chance to introduce another or to give the floor to someone who hasn't yet spoken. Something like this, perhaps: "Tom has been telling us that many of the exconvicts with whom he works are school dropouts who need brushup work in math and reading. Maxine gives the brushup before students drop out. Do you think that helps keep them in school, Maxine?"

If the Roundtable has a theme that is, if I've brought several people together who are interested in the same thing, whether it's art, music, religion, or the state of the economy I introduce the subject early and let them have at it. If the talk goes well, I interrupt as seldom as possible, usually only for the purpose of drawing in someone who hasn't been heard from.

If, on the other hand, the guests have varied interests, I

Self-deprecating humor is essential or you will come off appearing bossy.

frequently find it effective to call on each person to tell us what he or she is involved in at the moment. This assures that everybody will be included in the conversation. Even the shyest, most inarticulate person can become quite eloquent when talking about a pet project. It also guarantees the introduction of a variety of subjects, some of which are bound to inspire animated conversation.

And there are frequently surprises. You expect the writer to tell you about the book he's writing. Instead, you learn about writer's block. The painter wants to talk about jogging, and the physician about her acting class.

When the conversation is really rolling, let it roll. Don't guide or interrupt it unnecessarily. Just enjoy it. But be aware that what interests you doesn't necessarily interest everybody, and be alert to signs that interest is waning. One of these is the development of little separate conversational groups. They are inevitable occurrences' when someone holds the floor long and tediously. Best to interrupt that speaker and prevent the splintering of the table, but if you can't do that, bring the Roundtable back to a common subject by calling for attention, yourself.

I do this laughingly, with a bell, which has become my Roundtable trademark. Self-deprecating humor is essential or you will come off appearing bossy. Laugh and the world laughs with you, cry and you cry alone is a slogan to keep in mind. I usually introduce the bell by ringing it at the beginning of a Roundtable, warning with a laugh that, "This is to keep you all in line." Or something like that. Because of the bell, regulars at the Roundtable often help keep the conversation running smoothly. Someone may become a longwinded conversation—monopolizer that will not stop and one might say, "If you don't let someone else talk pretty soon, Pat is going to ring her bell." References to the bell have become an easy way for guests to remind each other it's time to yield the floor. I rarely ring the bell unless competing conversational groups have sprung up. Then I tap the bell lightly and return the conversation to the whole table. Or I say it is time to ask <u>The Question</u>.

THE QUESTION

<u>The Question</u> comes toward the end of lunch. It is always personal, and the same question is asked of each individual. I tried <u>The Question</u> originally because I found that some luncheons were totally intellectual. Guests left knowing what other guests thought about economics, prostitution, politics, and a host of other subjects but there was no emotional interaction. So, in fact, everybody left as they had come, strangers. And that wasn't what I had in mind.

The Question is designed to let guests reveal themselves emotionally after they've had time to become acquainted intellectually. If they want to, of course. Some guests will duck <u>The Question</u>. Or answer it frivolously. That's their privilege. I've found, though, that most guests are intrigued by <u>The Question</u>, eager to answer and hear the answers of others.

I have also had Roundtables at which <u>The Question</u> wasn't necessary. An emotionally charged, personal discussion sometimes naturally evolves from the conversation. Or one of the guests asked a searching question for me.

The Question comes toward the end of lunch. It is always personal, and the same question is asked of each individual.

Still, I like to be prepared with <u>The Question</u> before a Roundtable. Usually it's something that has emotionally intrigued or touched me. And I often answer <u>The Question</u> first, to set a pattern of honest, emotional openness for the others. Don't underestimate the courage that takes. You're making yourself totally vulnerable, and that may not be easy. Once I answered <u>The Question</u> and surprised myself by crying as I recalled an incident from my childhood.

Immediately, the atmosphere was charged with empathy, and as person after person answered <u>The Question</u>, there were more tears and a great sense of sharing. Had I allowed my own emotions to embarrass me, I would have cut others off from a unique and meaningful experience. As the first to answer <u>The Question</u>, you don't necessarily have to shed tears, but do shed the inhibitions that lead to prescribed behavior and conversation. Allow yourself to be vulnerable.

The kinds of questions I have asked as <u>*The Question*</u> *are:*

- Is there anything you would like to change about yourself?

- Do you believe in God?

- You have four months left to live. What would you want to do with that time?

- Do you consider yourself a powerful person?

- Is love important to you?

- What do you want to achieve in this life? Please explain.

- What sad event in your life became a motivating force?

- What is your first memory?

- Other than your birth family, what person from your childhood made a deep impression on you?

At one Roundtable, I asked, "What do you need to enhance your life?" Joan Baez was only one of those who answered. "Time to myself!" She explained, "I would like to be able to spend time alone, doing what I want, without condemning myself. That's really,

really hard to do after so many years. People expect things of me. I expect things of myself. I don't mean music. In music I seem to be able to handle demands without much problem. It's the political expectations that burden me. I feel guilty saying 'No. I want to study or spend time with my son, Gabriel.' I haven't been able to do that very successfully. And that's what I want to enhance my life. I want a sabbatical or whatever you wish to call it. I want to breathe a little bit."

As she elaborated, we were given an insight into the life of another person that none us could have experienced or imagined had it not been for her truthful response in answering The Question.

Janet Gray Hayes, the Mayor of San Jose, also wanted "Time! Time! Time!" to enhance her life. "Because I'm on a fast track, like a downhill skier. It's very enjoyable, I'm not bored. Mine is a very rewarding, challenging, demanding job. But never once this morning did I think that I would not come here this noon, because this is the way I recharge my batteries. It's refreshing to be with people who are not haranguing me or demanding things. I really am grateful for this opportunity to kind of stretch my mind with new ideas and new people and new experiences. So I'm recharging my batteries. And that enhances my life."

The Question at one Roundtable was "What are your anxieties?" Elayne Jones, an award-winning timpanist, responded. "I'm always anxious. As a black woman, I feel the need to be better than my white peers at everything from music to sports. It makes me very anxious." As she elaborated, we were given an insight into the life of another person that none us could have experienced or imagined had it not been for her truthful response in answering The Question.

There are usually no comments by others on the answer a

person gives to <u>The Question</u>. Far from being judgmental, those who share these revelations are grateful for a rare and privileged glimpse into another's inner being. By the time everyone has answered <u>The Question</u>, the room is usually still, but the quiet throbs with feeling. Anything more would be anticlimactic. I stand up and thank my guests for coming. Our Roundtable is over.

There are warm goodbyes, with much touching and hugging and cheek kisses. I no longer am surprised at the transformation of my guests. People who greeted each other stiffly, often as strangers, just two or three hours before, now part as friends, leaving some of themselves with others, taking something of others with them, to keep and cherish, perhaps for a lifetime. It is then, as my guests leave, that I think of Somerset Maugham's observation that "Conversation is one of the greatest pleasures in life." It is, indeed. And I know the conversation I have just been a part of will give me food for thought and inspiration for months to come. It is also the reason that, before long, I will find myself planning another Roundtable.

CHAPTER SIX

Sunday Supper

During the hot summertime of Waurika, Oklahoma, my mom (with her children helping) would take a wicker basket filled with fried chicken, cold biscuits, hand-churned butter, and jam to a nearby park for a Sunday Supper. There were cotton wood trees fanning us with their branches and a small stream nearby. We often invited those we met along the way to join us, and they usually did. Well you should have heard those conversations! We used old newspapers to cover the table. All the guests traveled with their own spoons, knives, and forks, we supplied paper plates and songbirds provided the music. Everyone had such a joyful time it was past bedtime when we toddled off to sleep. But not before some vanilla ice cream, hand-churned, was ready to be devoured at home. I felt like I'd died and gone to Heaven.

Our guests were always treated with respect, no matter their station in life or their circumstances. Thanks to those Sunday suppers, I have always valued the way a gathering can draw people out. After these kinds of get-togethers, one leaves the table feeling connected to others and to oneself, having learned something

***After these kinds of get-togethers,
one leaves the table feeling connected to
others and to oneself,
having learned something about life that
we didn't know before we sat down.***

about life that we didn't know before we sat down. Indeed, a lively meal can create deep memories that we carry with us forever.

The rules for hosting Sunday Night Supper are the same as those for Roundtable Luncheons, except for the menu and lighting. So much of life is lived around the family table: we tell stories, review the day, pass on traditions, grieve our losses, resolve differences, introduce new loves and celebrate holidays.

Nothing cements relationships or promotes laughter and connections with others quite so much as a relaxed, easy-to-prepare, family-style Sunday Night Supper. Good food and good conversation are unbeatable combinations. Include your school-age children in your Sunday suppers and the conversation. I guarantee you will learn things that will surprise you. When your son or daughter becomes an adult, you will find out how special your Sunday Night Suppers were to them and how quality time at the family table influences their lives. In the preparing and sharing of meals we imbued feelings that assist us in navigating our life path.

The menu can be as simple as a pot of stew, French bread, sweet butter and for dessert, ice cream with chocolate syrup. You can never go wrong serving ice cream and chocolate. A good stew is always a hit on cool evenings. The same is true of Texas Chili served with a crisp green salad and apple pie or some other fabulous sweet for dessert. Yummy!

I often use chafing dishes to keep foods hot and moist when friends gather for Supper. Chafing dishes are available in a wide variety of sizes. Some are made of copper, some of silver, and some of stainless steel. Some are electric, others heated with a flame. Other lower-cost chafing dishes are disposable, if you can believe it. A chafing dish can also come in a variety of different shapes. The most popular form is probably the rectangular chafing dish, as there seem to be more of these for sale than any other kind. But there are also round chafing dishes. Check online for rental companies in your community or borrow one from a neighbor.

Of course, your summer menu is much different than in colder months, unless you live in San Francisco. Mark Twain has often been quoted as saying "The coldest winter I ever saw was a summer I spent in San Francisco." I can verify that, having lived in San Francisco for forty years.

When entertaining in the evenings think candles, candles, and candles. Everything and everyone looks more attractive by candlelight. Candles add warmth, style and ambiance to any room in the home. Whether grouped for drama in the living room, clustered in candlesticks on the dining table, or nestled in a series of colored-glass votives on the mantel, tapered candles make everything look better—even that old living room chair everyone seems to own. You can never have too many candles. Just remember to light them. Before one Sunday Supper, a friend in charge of lighting the plethora of pillar candles I had placed on the supper table and mantel, forgot to light them. He remembered just as the doorbell rang and then he couldn't find matches. Fortunately, the first guest to arrive had a packet of matches and thus saved the night, *er*, the light!

Lighting can make a scene feel happy, sad, romantic, mysterious or dangerous— just as it can in your home.

Oh, and please, please, remove those thousand-watt bulbs your husband put in the light fixtures so he could see to work on the car. You might as well entertain in a parking garage. Every line in your face and the faces of your guests will be magnified and your skin will look sallow. The evening you had so carefully planned will end before it gets started.

The next time you go to a movie, pay attention to the way the director uses lighting to help create the mood in a scene. Lighting designer's work very closely with directors to build a scheme that adds to the drama and intensifies the emotions. Lighting can make a scene feel happy, sad, romantic, mysterious or dangerous—just as it can in your home. So, keep that in mind as you ready your home for a Roundtable, and don't forget to look up at the stars, the best light of all.

The following is a summary of A Sunday Night Supper before the Internet became an integral part of our lives. Having a computer glowing in your dining room was not the usual sight at that time. I wrote about it for the *San Francisco Examiner*:

Miniature white lights decorated my gated entry as well as the trees lining the path to the home I called the Enchanted cottage, lending a fairyland in-the-woods ambiance on a balmy Southern California kind of evening. Inside, the unexpected gleam of a computer screen contrasted with flickering candles and fragrant lilies.

"We're having a "virtual" supper," I announced, asking guests to sign in online. Humoring me, actor Danny Glover and his gallery-owner wife, Asake Bomani; author Merla Zellerbach with her fiancée, financier Lee Munson; Barry Minkin, a futurist from Stanford; and Emmy and Academy Award winning documentary filmmakers Catherine Ryan and Gary Weimburg, all logged on to the net.

Not recognizing him, writer Herb Gold asked Danny to repeat his last name. Smiling, the movie star once again pronounced Glover for the eminent scenarist who looked slightly abashed. Having a celebrity present gives a party added pizzazz, but it soon dissipates unless the person, like Danny, is down to earth and engaging.

"Does this virtual thing mean you aren't feeding us?" Merla asked quizzically, handing me several bottles of fine Zellerbach Estates wine. A veritable feast of gingered squash and apple bisque, followed by glazed Chilean sea bass served on potato puree with fermented black bean sauce, was in the offering. But first we were to connect; via the Internet to another group of Sunday diners I had met on AOL. This evening was an experiment to see if we could pull off a cyberspace Sunday Night Supper Club adventure. The other group, none of whom I knew, was to join us for dessert.

"I'm a virgin at this" Catherine Ryan said, attempting to e-mail Russ Mumford, host of the other party. When a private chat line opened there were messages from Bruce Cass, a wine writer and educator, Antea Ford Von Hennenberg, gourmet food promoter, architect Rob Cris, Davis Zweig, director of City Search, an online site, and Susan Fassberg, publicity manager of Thrive, an online health site.

"What a 90's way to meet a new group of people." Gary said. "Let's hope they're not related to Jack the Ripper."

After fooling around with my uncooperative computer, I left it to glow alone while I played catch up with in-the-flesh chums. Virtual reality could wait for The Ripper and cohorts. As soon as we took our places at an outdoor candle-lit table, surrounded by trees and overlooking a small waterfall, splintered discourse began. As if scanning radio frequencies, overlapping conversations eddied around me like the ocean tide. "Mayor Willie Brown finally got the message about cleaning up Golden Gate Park." "I'm worried about the melting ice cap, but this weather almost makes me forget." "How about the 49ers?" "There's no such thing as society now, only coffee shop aristocracy."

"We're having a 'virtual' supper," I announced, asking guests to sign in online.

In an effort to reclaim the table, so everyone could be included, I asked Asake if she's an artist. No, she said, but she promotes female artists in her gallery. Interjecting a comment, Danny showed devotion and respect, "Asake, You *are* an artist. Your life is lived artistically, that's an art form." She also wrote poetry and sings he noted.

As dialogue segued to dreams, the kind we have when we sleep, Asake told of dreaming about a friend she was on the outs with,

Barry stood, "I propose a toast; 'Here's to friends who won't let you drown.'"

and receiving a phone call from that person the next day revealing the exact same dream at the same time. Merla recounted her effort to find an ending for her book, *Love In A Dark House,* and having the answer come in a dream.

"I never dream." Lee said, making him a good listener.

Ever witty, Herb Gold commented that the males probably wouldn't mention the dreams they really have, of a girl clad in skimpy white cotton undies.

"I'll never forget a nightmare I once had" Danny allowed. In it he was drowning and friends, whose faces he recognized, were watching him go under for the third time. No one tried to save him. Awake, he reevaluated the people in his life, accepting responsibility too, and made changes.

There are often messages in our nighttime mental images that we should pay attention to, we thought. Perhaps nightmares represent that which we can't confront when wakeful, Gary said. Agreeing, I recounted ten years of terrifying dreams connected to the loss of my family because of betrayal. Awake, I couldn't deal with it.

Futurist Barry Minkin said he was at the Green Gulch Zen center near Muir Beach, when he got word his father had died, "I was in the perfect place to deal with loss." That night he dreamt his father was cushioned by ocean waves, cradled, soothed, happy. The consolation he got from that vision, gave him the strength to cope. Just as we began discussing Humanity 3000, my computer sounded an alarm, alerting us to the imminent arrival of online guests. "Before the virtual ones arrive," Barry stood, "I propose a toast; 'Here's to friends who won't let you drown.'"

My virtual guests? Not a Ripper in the lot.

CHAPTER SEVEN

Food for Thought

A few years ago there was a story in the *New York Times* about an elderly woman who was having dinner at a senior facility when she began to choke. Fortunately, the man for whom the lifesaving Heimlich maneuver was named sat one place away from her. The gentleman calmly got up from his chair and proceeded to save the woman's life

Keep that incident in mind when planning your Roundtable menu—it's too late to invite Dr. Heimlich to your luncheon salon, as he has passed on to that Great Table in the beyond.

One luncheon made me rethink my food menu. During the meal my guests wouldn't engage in the topics or react to the questions I suggested. I was confused and annoyed; what had I done wrong? It was an eclectic mix of interesting folks—a politician, a famous actor, two long-time friends, and a rabble-rouser who by his very nature could usually incite strong reactions, but not this time. Why had the conversation stopped like the proverbial ship hitting an iceberg?

It took me a few seconds to realize that dialogue stopper was no less than the food my guests were struggling to eat; broiled lobster tail. Well, duh. Have you ever tried to eat lobster and talk at the same time? Anyway, who would want to talk while chewing lobster with butter dripping off your chin? I learned a lesson about what to serve if I'm interested in Good Talk by making a social blunder I will forever remember.

When I asked friends about their experiences with foods that stop conversation I came up with a list and lots of stories (see list at the beginning of this chapter).

So there you have it. Send me your thoughts and your own personal list of foods that stop conversation.

Now, onto foods that *facilitate* conversation. Chef Keith Graber, who often cooks for my Roundtables, offers his insight on designing a menu that entices conversation from guests and allows them to easily maneuver through the meal-

"When creating your menu, it is important to select dishes that will encourage conversation. Avoid any dishes that might offer distractions or stifle your guests' ability to engage with one another. Choose menu items that are served complete and do not require additional sauces or toppings in a separate serving dish. Also, any foods that are messy or difficult to eat should be avoided. Never pass up an opportunity to add an interesting element or garnish to a dish. While simplicity is key to an elegant meal, exotic and fragrant additions like fresh herbs and toasted spices can stimulate the senses. Toasted cumin or cardamom and fresh herbs like tarragon or curry leaf will fill the room with fragrance that will be sure to get your guests talking. Visual aesthetic is always a significant factor in any impressive meal. A variety of colors and contrast will be sure to stimulate the senses and get people talking. Simple choices like choosing heirloom carrots or pairing green and yellow zucchini are easy ways to incorporate visual appeal in your food. Make a point to layer contrasting ingredients in each of your dishes. Seasonality can also play a big part in your menu design. There are many seasonal ingredients to take advantage of that will evoke past memories and feelings, which is sure to stimulate conversation. Our emotional connection to the foods we eat is incredibly strong and can often be intertwined with our thoughts and mood. It is also beneficial to include new ingredients in your meal. Learning is a key part of any healthy discussion. And discovering a new ingredient, dish, or cuisine can help

Foods That Stop Conversation

1. **French Onion Soup** "It's scary," a friend said. "I was at a dinner where French onion soup was served and that slippery cheese got stuck in my throat. The host had to call 911. That sure as heck stopped conversation."

2. **Fried Chicken** The best way to eat fried chicken is with your fingers. Save it for a family dinner or a picnic.

3. **Spaghetti** Save it for a meal when conversation isn't important...but there goes your self-esteem.

4. **Finely Cut Salads** They are too hard to eat.

5. **Raw Spinach** "I become so self-conscious trying to eat a spinach salad that I can't say a word," a friend said. " I know that greens will be stuck to my front teeth if I open my mouth," he laughed.

6. **Fancy Foods and Presentations** "Most of us talk with our hands so we should keep that in mind," an acquaintance volunteered. "The caterer at a luncheon in the home of a friend put a crystal goblet with melon balls in the center of the plate

and around the salad. That seemed odd, but then, wouldn't you know, while talking, my hands flew across my plate and, of course, hit the goblet. Melon balls and broken glass ended up in the food, on my dress, my neighbors dress, and across the table."

7. **Steak** Takes the focus off conversation and onto the food.

8. **Peanut Butter Anything** "Please," said a friend. "When I'm trying to talk I don't want peanut butter sticking to the roof of my mouth."

9. **Chop Sticks** Not exactly a food, but unless all your guests use them well or you live in Asia the conversation easily dissolves into complaints and fork requests because of this utensil

10. **Shrimp Cocktail** "Talk about a disaster!" a friend said. "I was at a black tie dinner, dressed like a Penguin and strutting my stuff, when the first course was served. I didn't know if I should use the little fork to my left or not. One fellow was dipping his shrimp into the sauce and going for it so I decided to do the same. What a mess. I dripped red sauce on my tux and splattered my date too. A bad choice for a formal dinner."

open up perspectives. Try challenging yourself by incorporating something new and unique on your next menu. Then research its culinary application to optimize the effect it has in your dish."

Keith has also kindly provided sample menus, please experiment with them, and most of all—have fun!

SAMPLE MENU 1:

First Course
Broiled Asparagus w/ Lemon Aioli & Fried Sage

Main Course
Champagne Poached Salmon w/ Heirloom Tomatoes
Spinach & Sweet Potato Frittata w/ Avocado Crema
Baby Kale Garden Salad w/ Apple Cider Vinaigrette

Dessert
Triple Silken Pumpkin Torte
Cinnamon Honey Crème Brulee

Note: Desserts should be extra special so guests can go all-out when eating it. A spectacular dessert is the crown jewel of a menu and sets the meals final mood.

SAMPLE MENU 2:

First Course
Baby Gem Lettuce Salad Cups w/ Cherve, Hazelnuts &
Roasted Beets

Main Course
Finger Sandwiches:
Ham, Brie & Pear
Avocado, Cream Cheese & Sprouts
White Cheddar, Arugula & Dijon

Mini Quiches:
Heirloom Leek Topped w/ Smoked Salmon Mousse
Butternut Squash w/ Fresh Basil

Dessert
Homemade Scones w/ Fresh Cream & Fig Jam
Assorted Petit Fours w/ Decorative Toppings

Here are a few some alternate menu items as well, to give you inspiration and examples of how much variety there is to serving a meal in courses!

Salads (can be either a first or main course)
• Roasted Golden Beets w/ Cherve, Toasted Pecans & White Wine Vinaigrette
• Frisee w/ Toasted Pepitas & Pomegranate Vinaigrette
• Butter Lettuce w/ Tomato, Avocado & Dijon Vinaigrette
• Organic Greens w/ Crispy Kale, Heirloom Carrots & Champagne Vinaigrette
• Massaged Kale w/ Lemon Zest & Grilled Avocado

First Course
• Grilled Shrimp & Avocado Salad Cups
• Burrata w/ Arugula & Fresh Figs
• Soft-Boiled Egg w/ Wilted Spinach & Crispy Diced Bacon
• Baked Avocado w/ Basil & Brie

Second Course
• Savory Palmiers w/ Goat Cheese, Sundried Tomato & Pine Nuts
• Potato Croquettes w/ Spicy Remoulade
• Risotto Cakes Stuffed w/ Cheese & Fresh Herbs
• Tuna Poke in Cucumber Cup
• Sriracha Devilled Eggs w/ Smoked Sea Salt

Main Course

- Poached Salmon Filet w/ Lemon & Fried Capers
- Grilled Tri-Tip w/ Horseradish Cream & Shaved Fennel
- Organic Chicken Breast w/ Basil Pesto Aioli
- Chicken Terrine w/ Tarragon & Pistachio

Sides (for main course)

- Orzo Pasta Salad w/ Shaved Parmesan & Grilled Vegetables
- Kale and Quinoa Salad w/ Butternut Squash, Cranberry & Walnuts
- Roasted Butternut Squash & Edamame w/ Sesame Vinaigrette
- Farro Salad w/ Feta & Toasted Pecans
- French Lentil Pilaf w/ Roasted Kabocha Squash

Desserts

- Gingerbread Cake w/ Orange Zest Crème Anglaise
- Poached Pears w/ Cardamom Shortbread
- Toasted Almond Semi-Freddo w/ Macerated Berries & Avocado Honey
- Stewed Winter Fruit w/ Vanilla Custard
- Coconut Panna Cotta w/ Lavender Wafers

A Select List of Historical and Current Roundtable Participants

Joan Baez · Folk singer, activist

Harvey Milk · American politician

Lorel Bergeron · Plastic surgeon

Jean Borgan · Psychic

Eldridge Cleaver · Former Black Panther, author of *Soul on Ice*

Jack Crowley · Union boss

Dr. Carl Djerassi · Inventor of the birth control pill

Daniel Ellsberg · *Pentagon Papers*

Dianne Feinstein · US Senator

Betty Friedan · Author of *The Feminine Mystique*, founder of the National Organization for Women, National Women's Caucus, and National Abortion Rights Action League

Abigail Van Buren · *Dear Abby* Columnist

Gordon Getty · Son of J. Paul Getty, composer, opera lover

Bill Graham · Rock impresario: Fillmore East, Fillmore West

Janet Grey Hays · Mayor of San Jose

Alex Haley · Author of *Roots*, a groundbreaking work

Aileen Hernandez · Urban consultant, second president of NOW

Warren Hinckle · Writer, rabblerouser

Sacheen Littlefeather · Native American who accepted an Oscar on behalf of Marlon Brando

Del Martin · Founder of Daughters of Belitis (she and her
partner of 50 years, Phyllis Lyon were the first to marry when
it became legal in California for gay couples to wed)

Jessica Mitford · British/American author of *The American
Way of Death*

Agnes Moorehead · American actress

Malvina Reynolds · Folk singer, composer; best known for
"Little Boxes"

Father Miles Riley · Catholic priest

Jean Shinoda Bolen · Psychiatrist, author

Dr. Mimi Silbert · Founder of Delancey Street, an organization
that rehabilitates criminals

Margot St. James · Former prostitute, founder of C.O.Y.O.T.E.
(Cast Off Your Old Tired Ethics)

Gloria Steinem · Feminist, founder of *Ms.* Magazine

Dr. Claude Steiner · Psychologist, author of *The Games People
Play*

Danielle Steel · Author

Shirley Temple Black · Most popular child star in history, U.S.
Ambassador to Ghana

Burl Toler · First Black NFL referee

Jessamyn West · Author of *Friendly Persuasion* (made into a
film with Gregory Peck)

Leone Whitaker Baxter · Businesswoman, political advisor

Jan Yanehiro · Television personality

Merla Zellerbach · Author of nine books, San Fransisco
personality

Steve Martin · Actor, banjo player

Mike White · Writer, actor, filmmaker (*School of Rock*)

Linus Pauling · Two-time Nobel prize winner

Nancy Pelosi · Politician and Speaker of the House of
Representatives

Anne Getty · Philanthropist, socialite, interior designer

Julia Hare · Author

George Davis · Attorney (Caryl Chessman case)

Elaine Jones · First Black timpanist with San Francisco Symphony

Sam Wasson · *New York Times* bestselling author

Paul Erdman · American economist, author

Melba Beals · Integrated Little Rock School

Sydney Goldstein · Founder of San Francisco City Arts & Lectures

Marcia Brandwynne · Television anchorwoman, producer, therapist

Reg Murphy · Publisher, business executive

Sandol Stoddard · Author of *The Hospice Movement*

Richard Tam · Designer

Gay Blackford · Disabled rights activist

Rollo May · Psychologist, author of *Love and Will*

Patricia Sun · Institute of Communication for Understanding

David Scheff · Author of *Beautiful Boy*

Jim Dunbar · TV star, KGO San Francisco

Ginetta Sagan · Human rights activist, founder of Amnesty International

Alfred Wilsey · Businessman, philanthropist

Delia Ehrlich · Urban consultant

Ann Gilbert Getty, Annie Plops, Betty Friedan

Gordon Getty, Julia Hare   **Attorney George Davis**

Dr Steiner, Janet Grey Hays

Bill Graham, Pat Montandon

Dianne Feinstein, Agnes Moorehead

Warren Hinckle, Del Martin

Pat Montandon, Alex Haley

Leone Baxter Whitaker, Ina Dearman, Shirley Temple Black, Merla Zellerbach

George T. Davis, Gay Blackford, Ken Washington

Paul Erdman, Janet Grey Hays   **Rollo May**

Sandol Stoddard, Daniel Ellsberg

David Scheff, Aileen Hernandez, Jim Dunbar, Ginetta Sagan, Alfred Wilsey

Melba Beals

Marcia Brandwynne, Reg Murphy

Linda McCallum, Rollo May, Patricia Sun

Sydney Goldstein, Pat Montandon

Steve Martin, Miranda July, Mike White, Sam Wasson

Dorthea Walker, Danielle Steel, Richard Tam, John Traina

Father Miles Riley, Elaine Jones

Father Miles Riley, Mimi Silbert, Eldridge Cleaver

**During the following years:
1973 · 1976 · 1977 · 1978**

Pat began hosting alumni Roundtables during the holiday season. Among the guests in 1982 were bright young children who were going on a Peace Trip to Russia with Pat. Each table (for over 300 alumni) was decorated in a Peace theme. At the end of the luncheon, held in a hotel ballroom, the children released Peace balloons over the city. Suddenly, without fanfare, the beautiful voice of Joan Baez enveloped the room with the classic carol "Silent Night," another unforgettable Roundtable moment.

Connie & Bob Lurie, Herb Gold & Donna Huggins

Jan Yanehiro, Delia Ehrlich, Beth & Jim Dunbar

Historic Dialogue from the Roundtable

Prepare to be amazed at the conversations engaged in by guests at Roundtables in:
1973 · 1976 · 1977 · 1978 · 1979 · 2020

"The more things change, the more they stay the same."
—JEAN-BAPTISTE ALPHONSE KARR

Sometimes what we perceive as a significant change is really not so significant, and vice versa. Or, a series of groundbreaking events can cycle back to a state eerily reminiscent of their beginning.

CHAPTER EIGHT

2020

Black Lives Matter

This book was written, edited, ready to be published when—*Zoom*—the Coronavirus enveloped the world in seemingly unending masked quarantine.Our mutual plight gave me pause about publishing a book regarding creating friends and influencing people, when we were hunkered down with bottles of sanitizer and wearing a mask. What was I to do? Then a friend sent me a text suggesting I have a remote gathering—perhaps through Zoom. "*Zoom*? What are you talking about?" intrigued, I soon found out—so now—read on and I will show you how I did it and how you can do it too.

And now to the current year, 2020 and the Black Lives Matter luncheon, because of the impact of COVID-19, I want to show you how easily one can put together a virtual Roundtable that, at the sunrise of *Recipes for Conversation*, shows how impactful and revealing conversation can be.

Please notice how this conversation begins and how freely all the guests have their say. Even though it was remote and therefore different from the usual Roundtable, my guests were open and honest. We broadcast the conversation over Facebook Live, allowing me to learn that it touched many of those listening by the depth, thought, and information the participants brought to the virtual table and into the world.

GUESTS

Rachel Skiffer • Dean of Khan Lab School, former attorney

Storm Jenkins • guns rights activist

Kennerly Clay • animal activist

Lisa Keels • retail worker

Mary V. Atkins • deaf & disabled telecommunications marketing manager

Kelly Dearman • Director of San Francisco In-Home Supportive Services Public Authority

PAT: *Rachel, I often think about you, and your two little children. All that's happening to the African American community affects everybody, but it affects people with children more than anyone. How you're dealing with all of this in terms of your family?*

RACHEL: *My husband is Black, but he's Jamaican-American. What is most interesting to me is seeing him embrace his Black-American-ness in a way he hadn't before. I was there the first time he was pulled over; we were shocked!*

PAT: *What was he pulled over for?*

RACHEL: *Being Black in a nice car. [laughs]*

PAT: *Oh my god! No!*

RACHEL: *He'd never had that experience before, and the trooper who pulled us over seemed shocked about what he came upon, versus what he expected. Apparently, he expected drug runners. Josiah was still a baby; it was cold and so I was in the back seat with him. The officer asked where we were coming from, and if the car was registered. My husband replied no it was a rental, and the trooper asked him why it was a rental, to which my husband asked why did it matter if it was a rental? And I thought "Oh, he's new to this, don't get us killed on the side of the road."*

Then the trooper peered in the back of the car and said, "Is that a baby?" and I said "Yes! There's a baby in here and it's very cold." I think he expected to see some drug runners in the car. He was so shocked he had to leave us a little to deal with his own racism. We were not what he expected at all.

PAT: *We make judgments about people all the time . . .*

RACHEL: *People are starting to understand the history of policing in the US . . . slave patrols and how law enforcement came to be in this country. I'm glad people are educating themselves. As far as my kids go, they're young enough that I'm focused on moving them up in terms of self-esteem, cherishing their blackness and their skin and their hair, getting them casually diverse books, just to register the everydayness so they don't feel like they are "other."*

PAT: *I've seen racism firsthand. Incidentally, or more than incidentally, my father was a preacher, and he invited African American people to his services—I'm talking about the 1930's! And they came! It created a big, big upset in the church. These so-called Christians, who don't live the life, should just shut up! That's what I think. Religion can be a horrific burden for people and show the easy way to the wrong way. In regard to what my father did, he was ousted from the ministry for inviting Black people to his services! So, you know, my family has suffered from racism too in that sense . . . he died not long after that.*

STORM: *If I could interrupt . . . I see myself as being the foil here, with a different perspective, but wanting to achieve the same thing. I'm a former law enforcement officer, a onetime Republican nominee . . . Am I getting kicked off yet? [laughs]*

PAT: *Of course not! We want your opinion.*

STORM: *Well then, I'm also gay, and every one but two of my nephews and nieces are Black. So, I bring a lot of different perspectives into my conversations. I was very interested listening to Rachel because what you went through was entirely sincere to you. I can almost imagine why an officer would stop an out-of-state rental in that course . . .*

I had one experience when I was 20 years old, working patrol and pulled over a car, and it really informed the rest of my life regarding race. This driver didn't do anything but make an illegal stop, so I pulled them over, and it was a Black man. Now that's just to inform the story. I go up to the car and I notice his hands on the steering wheel are very rigid, he's looking straight ahead and not at me. I ask for his license and such. He answered, but very robotically and tense . . . he informed me exactly what he was doing before he did it, such as reaching for his wallet. He was so tense, so I figured he had to be dirty. He knew the protocol too

well, why was he afraid?

I didn't think he was dirty in the sense that he was a bad guy, I just wondered why he was so nervous for someone getting pulled over for only a traffic violation. I ran his information he had not even a single ticket under his name. I asked him, "You know the program so well, are you an ex-cop or an ex-con?" and finally his shoulders relaxed. He looked at me for the first time and said, like I was the stupidest person to ever walk on two feet, "I'm from LA." I was bowled over. So, I said give me that ticket, it was the kind of ticket we were not allowed to tear up, but I tore it up anyway.

That really made me realize that even though I'm a nice guy, he's a nice guy, because I'm a cop he has just as much prejudice against me, which is just not good either.

PAT: *Well Storm, surely you can understand why a person of color would be afraid of you, I mean god, look at how many Black people have been shot to death or imprisoned for something so small . . .*

RACHEL: *If I may interject, I have a legal background, so the thing is that my husband did not do anything illegal to get himself pulled over. So, there's the probable cause aspect, "Well, why DID he get pulled over?" Say if I was running drugs, I wouldn't be in the shiniest, biggest vehicle you could find.*

STORM: *Oh, I believe you that he did nothing wrong, I'm pro-law enforcement, but I'm mostly pro-Fourth Amendment, and you don't have the right to stop someone just because you can. You just don't serve someone if they don't give you a reason, but it happens, unfortunately. Another major issue that never seems to be addressed enough is that the Black population of America has a high rate of crime, unemployment and economic problems, which I think is caused by school systems that have abandoned their inner-city schools. There is this immense amount of money that is not going to the school systems . . . students aren't engaged and encouraged enough. Whatever system that exists in the United States seems to be telling young Black children, you can't succeed. I ask you Rachel, do you think there is any greater failure than the US and how it treats its black students?*

RACHEL: *Yes, there are greater failures.*

KENNERLY: *There are so many complexities to the things that impact Black children and their opportunities, more so than other ethnicities and races, that go way beyond education. None of those other races were enslaved for hundreds of years and treated the way Black people were for hundreds of years and have not experienced the same level of persecution that black people have.*

KELLY: *I have a 24-year-old son and an 18-year-old daughter. My son, in addition to being Black, has hearing issues so it's always been really frightening for me for him to even go outside. Because he might not always hear what people are saying to him. Storm, when I was listening to you and your story of how you pulled over that man, you should know that we teach our kids that that is how they are to behave when they get pulled over.*

It's commonplace for my son to be in a store and be followed around. I mean there is this tax on being Black that makes it really difficult to just move in the world. What I've said to him is that if I can get him to 25 then his life expectancy will match that of everyone else. That is a huge burden to bear. So, when you were telling that story I was just thinking exactly, that's exactly what they're supposed to do. Every single move they make, they have to make sure the cop is okay with it. We get pulled over for simply standing there, we get shot at because we are jogging. We get killed because of the color of our skin.

My husband is a cop, and I know that a majority of officers are good officers. The majority of people are good people, but I think it must be something in the training about Black and brown people in particular, just how they are perceived. With that affectation we are already in a negative place, there's already the expectation that we have done something wrong.

With a white person, it's "Oh they just made a mistake," with Black people, it's "You've clearly done something wrong and you need to prove that you are fine vs the opposite."

STORM: I can tell you Kelly it's not the training itself, when you get out onto the street, things become different. If you have a violent altercation with a person who happens to be a Black man, you are naturally going to be wary of men that are younger, stronger, and more fit than you. Officer safety is a really important part of our training.

RACHEL: I think what needs to happen is we go back to community policing and get back to officers knowing who is in their neighborhoods. Walking their beats. Police should know their communities and the communities should know them back.

PAT: How can we make that happen?

RACHEL: We re-prioritize, there are communities out there that have done this before and seen crime decrease. There are these sexual harassment trainings that work because when you feel safe, sexual harassment actually happens less. People sort of police each other and there's an expectation that it will be followed through and dealt with. We can work that system with community policing, possibly.

PAT: So, what can we do to make these changes happen? Lisa?

LISA: When this all happened with George Floyd it really hit home for me, as I'm born and raised in the south. It brought up a lot of my past and hit me in a way that crushed my soul. Seeing it happen over and over again, it's like, can somebody please say something? Can somebody open up? Can somebody do anything to make this stop?

LISA: As a Black woman in the south, I know what racism is, sometimes it's subtle, sometimes it's blatant. It's a cashier following me around the store, it's when I worked in retail and some people would not want to put the money directly into my hand. As if my Blackness would transfer to them. No one has ever run up to my face and called me the n-word, it's just the actions of people around you. It's the stigmatism that comes with the skin color.

God gave me this skin color, he gave us this skin color, maybe we're supposed to teach the world how to be. That's sad, but hey, if somebody has got to teach you, somebody's got to teach you. We don't have a violent mindset, like some think we do, I've always just wanted to talk with people I've had confrontations with. I feel like there's not a lot of communication because there's not a lot of people who want to be involved. People who don't want to talk to me because they think I'm not articulate, that's their problem. People who don't want to be in the same place as me because they think I'm going to do something, again, that is their problem, that's not my problem. We don't care enough for each other.

PAT: Don't you think that's true across the board? We talked about community and a new way of policing, when we don't know our neighbors! I certainly don't know mine! It's a ridiculous situation that we've allowed to fester.

LISA: Yes, I believe that because I live in an apartment and I know my neighbors, or at least how loud they are, hey I'm loud too though. I don't care that you're white and you're noisy, it's just the point of it is respect.

PAT: I keep repeating myself, how are we going to change it darlin'?

LISA: We have to respect each other; we have to find that thing that brings about respect. Look, I have to be honest with you, I am so far from the end of the spectrum here. I'm not saying this to be funny, but I'm talking to a law officer, a lawyer, I'm talking to people I wouldn't normally interact with on a day to day basis, but at the same time it's not about what you do as a job, it's about who you are. I'm here because I was invited and have a voice and something to say, it doesn't matter what I do, what matters is my heart. I respect each and every one of you for being involved and being part of the conversation that not only affects me, it affects you as well. I don't have any children, so I don't know what that impact would be on my child. I would probably be scared to death! I told Kennerly that I was afraid to go around the corner to the Dollar Tree because I didn't know if I was going to be harassed by a police officer, a white person in general, or a Black person confronting me about Black Lives Matter. I didn't want to be harassed by anyone; I just want to be myself. I just want to live my life. I don't want to be afraid to go outside.

PAT: You shouldn't have to be, but you know, you said "We're all so accomplished." Darling, I grew up very, very poor, we were on welfare. I barely got a high school education, but I've overcome all that. I've seen some racism firsthand. Incidentally, or more than incidentally, my father was a preacher, and he invited African American people to his services— I'm talking about the 1930s! He

> *I didn't want to be harassed by anyone; I just want to be myself.*

had not one prejudiced bone in his body, and they came! It was a big, big upset in the church. These so-called Christians, who don't live the life, should just shut up! That's what I think. Religion can be a horrific burden for people and show the easy way to the wrong way. In regard to what my father did, he was ousted from the ministry for inviting Black people to his services! So, you know, my side of the family has suffered from racism too in that sense . . . he died not too long after that. He kept saying "I did the right thing." He was an enormous influence in my life. I feel strongly about these issues and want to do whatever I can to change the environment around us all.

Mary, you go ahead, because I've got to cough, but I don't have the virus! Thank God.

MARY: *Hi everyone, I'm in Tulsa, Oklahoma, I'm a little bit unproud of that right now. I spent every summer up in Mississippi, on my uncle's farm. You know, he would buy groceries for his farm workers, because they had different prices, based on what you looked like . . . and he wanted them to get a fair price on groceries. If they had bought them themselves, they wouldn't have gotten that. When I was in San Francisco I was blessed to hear Jane Elliott speak about her Blue Eye/Brown Eye experiment, and that brought home the fact that we don't even know how racist we are. She brought up things like nude stockings, flesh-colored crayons, things that we weren't even aware how racism played a part in their creation. I don't have any perspective yet on what we can do to change all this, but every morning and evening I ask for the ability for all people to be compassionate, kind, patient, and respectful with their own self and others and I don't have a clue how to make that happen but that's what I pray for.*

PAT: *Well let's answer your prayers here if we can! [laughs]*

KENNERLY: *I read something recently about white people being very indignant with other white people about "not getting it," or not getting it in the "right way." It really spoke to me because if* *people are authentically trying to "get it" or be in the conversation and listening, we should be more patient and generous with each other. This is not easy for everybody. It shouldn't be white people dissing other white people for "not getting it" or being righteous about them not getting it fast enough.*

LISA: *That's right, Kennerly, you can't jump on somebody because they don't understand, that's what I meant too when I talked about respect. This is the time for us to teach each other and have a safe space to do that in. I can't make you respect me, but I can show you respect so I can understand where you're coming from, so you can understand where I'm coming from, and we can understand each other. This is how we learn from one another.*

LISA: *I was raised in an environment where the young sit underneath the old, because they could teach us things. But don't think just because I'm young I don't know anything! We can learn from each other. It doesn't take a village to raise a child, it takes a village to raise a community, it takes a village to raise a standard, to raise love and awareness. My priest said, "Love thy neighbor as you do yourself."*

RACHEL: *Can I add? Mary said something really interesting, my sense is the root of a lot of this reckoning is that many white people still need to understand how racist this country is. Even if you don't feel that you have hate in your heart, it could be something that you think is neutral that is actually racist. Things like Band-Aids drive me nuts, there is also the belief in the world, and particularly the US, about the inherent criminality of Black people and the inherent "super-naturalness" of Black people. Like the belief that we don't feel pain.*

Back when I could get a pedicure, I would always say specifically, "It hurts if you cut me," because there are these studies that say if you go to the hospital and you're a Black person, they're not going to give you the pain medication you need. They're going to under-treat you because there's this myth in America that Black people are superhuman. One of the reasons that Black people are not having this opioid crisis, is that white doctors wouldn't prescribe pain medication to Black patients.

PAT: No!

RACHEL: We won on that one!

STORM: *Rachel, when you use the term racism, do you define it only when there is hostility or a negative approach towards someone, or could it be more of a lack of understanding?*

RACHEL: Right, that's what I was saying. I guess I should define racist, some of it is systemic right? It's systems of power. Polaroid back in the day had this system, there was this white woman they would use as a model to check the color-readiness of Polaroid photos. So, whenever you would take a picture of a Black person, they'd turn out green or purple. It just didn't work! And so, the thinking went, "Oh no, it's so hard to take pictures of Black people!" but it's like, no! You built the film to not see us. It's not like people are trying to take horrible photos of Black people, it's something that was built into the system.

STORM: Is there an element of it that is just uninformed and ignorant rather, I speak for myself, when I'm accused of it [racism], it doesn't help. If I'm told I'm unaware or uninformed or maybe there's something that I want to understand. When Lisa was talking about the South, it reminded me of when I was in my 20s doing business in Alabama, and what I call racism, down there it's called "being Southern." It was like White people can walk on that side of the street; Black people can walk on that side of the street. I became informed of what that is.

I see so much division, we're focusing on the worst police officers on the world and the worst Black young men in the world, who are doing things that don't represent everybody else. It has polarized us. We focus on one bad cop, and 3 other bad cops who I think were worse than the one that had his knee on George

Floyd's neck, because they sat by and did nothing . . . that's not
a representation of the other 800,000 police officers.

RACHEL: But this is what I'm saying, I'm talking about one:
systems; and two: the racism that all of us carry because we grew
up in this country. It's not about using the n-word or separating
water fountains, we know that's bad, everyone now that saw
segregation thought it was bad. What we don't understand is
people who are going to force a belief onto another people
because they think Black people are stronger or I am going
to follow this person around in the store because what I don't
understand about US history is that as soon as slaves were free,
they changed the laws. They said if you weren't working, that was
a crime and they could put you in jail. So yes, they're free, but
then all of a sudden you start the criminality of Black people.

What I think we need to do as a country is understand
our systems, the belief that makes it okay to be sort of gently
prejudiced, if you don't like the term racist. What are systems that I
participate in that perpetuate some of this injustice? This shaming
that white people do of each other for not being aware enough, I
call it the "Woke Olympics." It doesn't help anybody, I think also
questioning Black people's Blackness, that's not helpful either. We
all have to get a real deep understanding of the racism in the air
we breathe, the water we drink, and the systems we participate in
that we don't even think about.

STORM: Like when planning a meal for Black friends . . . I wonder
do they know what they're doing? Not just with Black people, but
with any category of people that you're not a part of. You make
unconscious assumptions.

PAT: Well I did that once! [laughs]

With Alex Haley I had "down-South" food made for him,
because I knew he loved it! He was at a Roundtable, I served
collard greens, and black-eyed peas . . . I love it! He loved it
too . . . but now that I look back at it, I'm thinking, was that a bad

thing to do? I've done a lot of things like that, from my heart, not knowing it was something that could be considered outrageous.

STORM: *Our generation is a little different, my father had this expression, his highest form of compliment was, "Well she's a great broad!" I said that about Pat a little while ago, and I had like 40 people on Facebook saying, "Well you can't call her that!" and I said, "But she is!" She's great person.*

PAT: *Storm, I am a dyed-in-the-wool feminist, but we must pick our battles, or we grow tired and tiresome and the battle is lost.*

I once lived in Selma, Alabama, and I had this African American girl who came to do my ironing, which I loved because I could never iron a shirt and never would! One day she came when it was raining. She arrived soaked to the bone, and the dogs in the neighborhood were yapping at her ankles, as they always do. I said, "You don't have to put up with that! Why don't you give those dogs a kick or something? They're always yapping at your ankles!" She said oh no she couldn't do that; the white folks would put her in jail if she did such a thing. I said surely not! After I got her settled in some warm dry clothes, I went to the police department, complaining about the actions of the dogs in Selma. They just gave me the brush off, but that never left me . . . I just saw so much when I was there, such as segregated seating. I just took it for granted, and I think we do up to a point, till our consciousness is raised, until we realize the inequities in our society and put a stop to it. I think that takes a lot of thought and maturity, understanding and education. We should all educate ourselves and each other.

RACHEL: *Someone once said that people are afraid Black people want revenge. No, we just want*

> ***I am a dyed in the wool feminist, but we must pick our battles, or we grow tired and tiresome and the battle is lost.***

equality . . . white nationalist protestors have been caught on camera looting and being violent, knowing Black Lives Matter protestors would be blamed for it. Because people understand the system. The same way that woman in Central Park was harassing that very peaceful bird-watching man. She understood that if she said there was a Black man "harassing" her in the park, he'd be arrested or at worst he'd be physically harmed. At the end of that day, we just want it to be fair. A lot of it is that we have our own experiences with police, and people are like "Well this is fair." There are people that are like, "No! this is fairer!" That's why these conversations are helpful, you get a glimpse into other people's worlds.

RACHEL: It's interesting to look at the map of the west after elections, and some cities that were red before, they're always blue. My guess is that those different people come together, and it's hard to hate people you know. It's hard to hate people whose stories you understand, but when we are incredibly segregated, that's when I think all of this hatred grows. What we have in common can really help build to having conversations where we can change things.

STORM: When I meet someone new, I try to find one thing in common. If you have even one thing, like a hobby, then suddenly you're friends. You're both the same about this one thing, different as we are. It breaks down those walls.

LISA: We can understand each other on such a level, that it changes the world. It's not because I'm black, it's because were all human. We all have a heart, we all have a mind, we want to survive, we want to be here on this planet, and enjoy each other. What will we leave behind for future generations? We need to open our hearts, minds, and ears and start listening to each other.

CHAPTER NINE

1973

Warm Fuzzies and Cold Pricklies

Any good cook will tell you that you shouldn't try out a new recipe on guests. But when your recipes are for conversation and the ingredients are people, you have no choice. You can't serve the same conversational menu, Roundtable after Roundtable. That could get boring. When you add the unknown, anything can happen and frequently does.

Sometimes it is captivating. I invited Malvina Reynolds, composer and singer, to one Roundtable. With a face framed by white hair, she beamed love and charm. Malvina's songs always make an important statement, like the one about "Ticky Tacky Houses" which is her most famous. So because of her music, I rather expected her to make an important statement or two. But she didn't say a word. No matter how many times I directed the conversation to her, she just smiled and passed it quietly along to someone else. I didn't know how to involve her.

And then, between courses, she stood and said, "I prefer to talk with music." She had brought her guitar! She took it out of the case and played a song about how children have to be taught to hate

Any good cook will tell you that you shouldn't try out a new recipe on guests. But when your recipes are for conversation and the ingredients are people, you have no choice.

"carefully taught." We'd just been talking about that subject, and once she had finished singing, there was no more to be said. She'd made the final statement, the most eloquent statement of the day.

So the unknown can be surprising and delightful. Or it can skirt disaster and keep a hostess on her toes. This happened at one Roundtable that started out congenially enough as we remembered the late Eric Berne, the psychiatrist who founded Transactional Analysis. The conversation began between Joan Baez, who had once been in private and group therapy with Berne, and Claude Steiner, a psychiatrist who had worked with Berne closely

GUESTS

Joan Baez • Folk singer, composer, political activist

Vilma Martinez • Lawyer, head of the MexicanAmerican Legal Defense Fund

Claude Steiner • Psychologist, author of *Scripts People Live*

Paul Erdman • Economist, author of *The Crash of '79, The Last Days of America*

Marcia Brandwynne • TV news anchorwoman, dark-haired, bright, and articulate

Janet Gray Hayes • Mayor of San Jose, California

Reg Murphy • Newspaper editor, San Francisco *Examiner,* formerly Atlanta *Constitution*

Gordon Getty • Opera singer, son of J. Paul Getty, computer expert

Julia Hare • Co-founder of the Black Think Tank and radio talk show host

in the development of Transactional Analysis and, since Berne's death, had continued developing the theory.

Like Eric Berne, Claude Steiner had written several books. In one of them, *Scripts People Live,* he tells a captivating tale about the days when everybody had a bag of Warm Fuzzies. People gave out Warm Fuzzies freely, and everybody who received one felt warm and fuzzy all over. Although each bag seemed to have an endless supply of Warm Fuzzies, people began to worry that they would run out, and so they began exchanging Cold Pricklies and saving their Warm Fuzzies. Cold Pricklies made everybody feel cold and prickly all over, and so the world became a less happy place than it had been when Warm Fuzzies were abundant.

Warm Fuzzies were given spontaneously and generously at that luncheon, but the ambiance was prickly too, with some strong disagreements and sharp exchanges. By the time it was over, I felt as if I had been steering a ship through choppy seas. Disagreement was evident almost as soon as guests were seated, when Vilma Martinez interrupted Eric Berne's warm reminiscences with her own memory.

Vilma is a bright, young attorney who directed the Mexican American Legal Defense Fund, which fights oppression and discrimination on behalf of the Latino community.

VILMA: *Every time someone mentions Eric Berne, I think of a lawsuit I once handled, representing a Black man who wanted to be an airline steward. He wanted the job because he was being laid off as a Pullman porter. But in those days, the policy was to hire only female stewardesses. Well, when I started researching the law, I came across a case that had been decided earlier, called* Vias vs. Pan Am. *Pan Am defended their policy of hiring only women as stewardesses by calling Dr. Eric Berne to the stand. And Dr. Eric Berne testified that in the air, people experience claustrophobia and a sense of fear and anxiety and frustration and that women are better equipped to deal with these* *things than are men. Therefore it was perfectly proper that only women should be stewardesses. I'm happy to report that Pan Am lost the case.*

REG: *How long ago was that?*

VILMA: *Oh, let's see, maybe eight years ago.*

CLAUDE: *I remember that. Eric brought it to a seminar to discuss. He wanted to know what others thought of his testimony. In those days we were just becoming aware of sexism, and we were divided about it. Some agreed with him, and some said "No, it was wrong." What he said, that is.*

JOAN: *Eric Berne was totally nonpolitical. I was very young when I started therapy with him. About 19 or 20. And I was really neurotic and mixed-up and lost. But very clear about my politics. I have been so long as I can remember. So I was politically active while I was in therapy. I was living in Carmel then and took part in Carmel's first demonstration against the war in Vietnam. And while we were doing our little number in the park, I saw Eric Berne walk past. So the next time I went in to see him, I asked him what he thought of the demonstration. He said everybody looked pretty scruffy. Then I asked him what he thought about the war, and he gave me the domino theory. I said, "My God! You're a political moron." And he agreed. In spite of that, I went on with him in therapy for eight years. Once in a while, something political would come up in group, and we'd have a huge explosion. Then he'd ask me to just keep quiet because what we were doing wasn't about politics.*

PAT: *Did he help you? He must have if you continued for so long.*

JOAN: *Absolutely. When I went in, finally, and told him that I didn't think I needed therapy any longer, I also told him that in spite of the things we disagreed about, he had been a tremendous help. And I thanked him. And then he thanked me for* *everything I had brought to him.*

CLAUDE: *So you had a nice feeling.*

JOAN: *I had a great feeling!*

I thought that a good note on which to close our discussion of Eric Berne and get on to another subject. For one thing, I wanted to discuss Paul Erdman's book, *The Crash of '79*, which had come out a couple of years before, but which people were still discussing. It was a work of fiction, but people read it as prediction and were frightened by it. Marcia Brandwynne had just come back from Las Vegas with a story of how the book had unnerved her father's widow. I asked her to tell us about that. She looked up at Paul Erdman with her expressive big brown eyes, and he looked back at her expectantly through his rimmed glasses.

MARCIA: *Well, I was in Las Vegas because my father died there. We were sitting around in the traditional Jewish mourning, and there's nothing to talk about except things that are going on, and what was going on in Las Vegas was that everybody had been reading your book, Paul, and it has started an amazing, rolling movement to the point of panic.*

PAT: *I was fourteen when my father died. Death had never been dealt with in a very upfront manner in our family, even though my father was a minister and had presided at many funerals. So there wasn't any mutual support when my father died. The family was terribly fragmented, each into their own grief. And I began to shake. I would shake so much at night that the whole bed would be shaking, and I would have to get up and light a fire in the stove and put on a coat. And I'd still shake. I still shake that way when I'm under a great deal of tension. But I remember once a funeral my father held for a member of the church whom*

I considered a very dear friend. And I wanted to go. My mother said I couldn't; children didn't go to funerals. I wouldn't give up. I was about seven. I pleaded and insisted and demanded. Finally she said, "What if Brother John were to rise up out of his coffin and say, 'Boo!' to you? Wouldn't that scare you?" That was a silly thing to say to a child. And I said in answer, "I'd just say 'Boo!' right back to him." But I didn't get to go to the funeral.

JULIA: *We used to play those games, too.*

JOAN: *Dr. Kubler Ross writes and lectures about death and dying. She's talked with patients who had died and then been revived, and they all had similar experiences. They went through a dark tunnel and then came into bright light to meet someone they knew who had died or some religious figure.*

CLAUDE: *It's curious, isn't it? Light has always been a symbol of something mystical and eternal whereas darkness is the symbol for bad and evil.*

JULIA: *Martin Luther King decided he wanted to change that, and that was the beginning of "Black is beautiful."*

PAT: *I had no idea that was the beginning.*

JULIA: *I remember hearing him speak on the subject, and he ended up saying, "Black is beautiful." It was spontaneous, I think. And it caught on. That was the beginning of consciousness rising on the way black is used in a negative sense. You've been "blackballed" from a club. It's a "black day." You're in a "dark mood." People wear black at funerals when they're sad. But when they are getting married, they wear white. And the hospital's cleanliness is white.*

Light has always been a symbol of something mystical and eternal whereas darkness is the symbol for bad and evil.

As we talked of black and its changing connotations and of Blacks and their continuing struggling for equal rights, I thought of another minority, the gays, whose fight against discrimination was tearing San Francisco apart. In the midst of the San Jose fray was the mayor, Janet Gray Hayes, who had come late to lunch and had said practically nothing since she arrived.

In her tailored suit, Janet looked very businesslike, composed and ready for anything. But also tired. I knew there had been a confrontation in San Jose the night before and wouldn't have been surprised if she hadn't shown up for lunch. Had she come to the Roundtable because she wanted to escape the problems in San Jose for an hour or two? Or because she wanted to talk about them with friends? There was only one way to find out. I asked her.

JANET: *I just feel really battered and bruised. I've spent the morning trying to recover.*

GORDON: *Some of us don't know the whole story.*

JANET: *Well, we passed a gay pride resolution in San Jose a few weeks ago. We passed it on a four to three vote. I was the swing vote. The other three votes in favor had been in place for the three years that I have been mayor. But I hadn't made up my mind.*

CLAUDE: *About homosexuality?*

JANET: *Yes, about homosexuality. My background is psychiatric social work. And I had been trained that homosexuality was a mental problem caused by a castrating mother and a weak father and all that. But then there was the Anita Bryant brouhaha in Florida. And the psychologists and psychiatrists and the Public Health Association all did an aboutface on homosexuality. They stopped calling it a mental illness and recognized it as a lifestyle that people have because that's the lifestyle that they find better for them for whatever reason. So this was surfacing in San*

*Jose, and I thought I'd better update, learn what had changed
the expert's minds. I started reading and talking to people. I
was particularly impressed by a thesis I read by a human rights
commissioner. I began to see this as a human rights issue. So
I went to the Gay Community Church. And the feeling in that
church was one of such love and caring, in sharp contrast to
the City Council meeting last night, which was overflowing with
people, most of them Fundamentalists who wanted to rescind our
Gay Pride resolution. The chambers were full, the cafeteria was
full. And in that entire crowd there were maybe eight gays, who
were also Born Again Christians. And there was so much hate
there against them against all gays. They were denounced, they
were compared to murderers and rapists and child molesters. This
morning I called the Reverend of the Gay Church and told him
how proud I was of the gays because they handled themselves
with such dignity in the face of all this hate. They stood up and
said, "We are Christians too. We are born again. We have a
right to our way of life." They didn't lose their cool. I was truly
impressed.*

JOAN: *You should be proud of yourself too.*

For a minute all conversation stopped. Janet Gray Hayes was fighting back tears. She touched each eye with a tissue and breathed
deeply. Then smiled.

JANET: *This isn't what people saw last night. Last night I was in
perfect control, and everyone said so. I conducted the meeting
with dignity, and when the mob got out of hand, I said, "We're
going to recess if you can't come to order." But afterward . . .*

MARCIA: *Afterward wasn't on the news.*

JANET: *Well, as mayor and as the swing vote, I was the focal
point of so much hostility. Mind you, during the meeting we had*

tried to reach a compromise. We had changed our original resolution from Gay Pride to Human Rights. But that didn't satisfy them. And afterward they followed me into the restroom. They followed me out to the parking lot. They really battered me verbally. Never have I experienced the feeling of mass hatred that I experienced last night. And I've seen a lot of hatred in recent years. Blacks against white, and browns against whites, and whites against browns and whites. But last night it was middle class, white Christians my own people, I'm a devout Methodist coming off the blocks at me, demanding that I do something that I know is wrong.

JULIA: *Christians went to Africa and brought us here as slaves.*

MARCIA: *What you did was brave and right, and we're all proud of you. But San Jose is a city that everybody knows would take an intolerant view of homosexuality, so perhaps any political analyst would say that what you did could be politically damaging.*

JANET: *People saying that have been on the phone all morning. Those people are unforgiving. They're talking recall. My city manager called and said, "I've seen three council members recalled for less." And I said, "Well, if it happens, I'll go skiing next year." My minister called and said, "You have dug your own political grave."*

JOAN: *I'm sure you have a tremendous amount of support out there. They just weren't there last night. They don't realize the hatred.*

MARCIA: *And there are also antigays who are quite rational and decent.*

Through all this the Mayor of San Jose had been fighting tears, and she had lost. Small wonder. She had been through a rough night and morning. Her political future was at stake. She had faced raw, naked hatred. Few of us are called on to do that. But she wanted to tell us what it had been like, where she had been. She swallowed, wiped her eyes, and looked at Joan.

JANET: *While the phone calls were coming in this morning a million phone calls I was trying to pull myself together, and I put on your record "Miracles." Or maybe that's just the name of the song, not the record. But it was so true. You were singing about the sun comes up in the east every morning, and that's the important thing. That's the miracle. And after last night, after all the hatred, after that tough, tough meeting, I needed that perspective.*

Janet could no longer talk through her tears, so she stopped trying. I wanted to say something comforting, but before I could speak, Vilma spoke, punctuating her words with sharp movements of her hands.

VILMA: *You know, as a bleeding heart, I work in a bleeding heart organization every day and support a lot of bleeding heart causes. I work with the NAACP Legal Defense Fund, and I'm on the board of the NOW Legal Defense Fund, and I run the Mexican American Legal Defense Fund, and I know how tough it can be. But I think, Mayor, if you want to be mayor, or if you want to be something bigger, then you've got to do it and stop this, this falling apart. That's what they expect a woman to do. You've got to get in there and fight and keep fighting.*

PAT: *But she needs to be able to fall apart somewhere. She needs to get some comfort.*

PAUL: *That's right.*

MARCIA: *We all need support.*

VILMA: *I disagree with you 100 percent.*

REG: *I don't have any doubts that she'll get up and start walking again.*

JOAN: *What are you saying, Vilma? Are you saying that it's just not proper etiquette to fall apart at the Roundtable? Or are you saying you shouldn't fall apart period? Because you named all those organizations you've been involved with and how tough it is to fight for those issues that have been around forever. So which are you saying? Not to fall apart here or not to fall apart at all?*

VILMA: *Not to fall apart.*

REG: *I think you're using the wrong expression. She's not falling apart.*

VILMA: *Well, the issues are much more complex than gay rights, frankly. You know, the tension among the Hispanics Mexican Americans, Puerto Ricans, Cubans, et cetera are incredible. There's going to be a hard fight in there before we work them out. And part of my fight is that I'm a woman, and Hispanics do not readily accept the lead of a woman. But what I'm trying to say is, the road is very difficult. You've got to stay in there, and you have to fight. But I think if you want to be a politician, you've got to compete as a politician. And to succeed as a politician, you've got to act rather than indulge your personal health. Margaret Mead has always said that.*

JANET: *I reserve my right to be a human being.*

VILMA: *I'm not saying you shouldn't reserve that right. I'm just questioning where you should exercise that right.*

But what I'm trying to say is, the road is very difficult. You've got to stay in there, and you have to fight.

JOAN: *She's been involved in some very trying experiences politically before. And last night she was a pillar of strength. But I think it finally gets to be too much. Really it does. I know.*

REG: *There's a timetable here. You get battered one evening, and it takes a certain amount of time before you can walk again. I've been through that kind of battering. I think probably everybody has to one degree or another. Where you just have to collect the parts of yourself from all over the God damned house and put them back together.*

Janet had an appointment here today, and she came. She could have stayed home and slobbered all over the house. But I'm really glad she came here. And if I'm picking politicians, I'll take a human first. Please! And if she's going to fail at that job because she's going to be a little bit more human, then bully for her!

Joan Baez and Claude Steiner were both rising from their chairs. Were they leaving? We hadn't even had desert. But they weren't leaving. They were heading around the table toward Janet.

CLAUDE: *I want to give you a kiss and a great big hug! May I?*

JOAN: *I do too. Because I'm really proud of you.*

CHAPTER TEN

1973

Warm Fuzzies, Part 2: *How to Survive a Kidnapping*

I would have liked to report that after the Warm Fuzzies Janet Gray Hayes received, Warm Fuzzies were the order of the day. But that's not the way it happened. Each Roundtable takes on a character of its own, I've discovered, depending on the personalities of those who sit around it and how they interact. This particular Roundtable had Warm Fuzzies at its center, but there were Cold Pricklies lurking around the edges that kept popping up.

VILMA: *Reg, both you and I have worked with the Archbishop on projects, such as sending underprivileged children to summer camps, which I feel strongly about. I supported it with my own money, and I'm not a rich woman by any means. But I was upset, Sunday, to read in your newspaper that piece by Archbishop Quinn on preborn life.*

REG: *On what?*

VILMA: *What he called preborn life. That's quite a term, isn't it? It really means no choice for women, no abortions. Unborn life takes precedence over a woman's life.*

JULIA: *Was there no reply for balance?*

VILMA: *There was no reply.*

GORDON: *Will there be?*

REG: *No.*

MARCIA: *Why not?*

REG: *That was a personal opinion. If we haven't established our impartial position by now, then we're just hopeless. What Archbishop Quinn had to say has nothing to do with the policy of the paper.*

VILMA: *And in the same issue of the* Examiner/Chronicle, *I read an editorial favoring a San Francisco tradition of allowing certain private clubs to have exclusive use of certain public lands. A yacht club, for instance.*

JULIA: *Why would your paper take that position?*

REG: *What's being questioned here? The practice or the position of the paper?*

Controversy can frequently be instructive. Or it can become antagonistic, which is what happened at this time. If I let it go on, people were apt to go home with acute cases of indigestion. And anyway, there was something I really wanted to hear Reg Murphy talk about. So I changed the subject.

PAT: *Reg, you were one of the first kidnap victims in the present escalating wave of kidnappings and other crimes. And I know you've been telling people since how to survive a kidnapping in case it should happen to them giving lectures and seminars. How did it happen in your case?*

REG: *Well, it was back in '74. I was the editor of the Atlanta Constitution in Georgia. These two men were supposed to have a fellow who would donate 300,000 gallons of fuel oil to charities, and I was supposed to pick the charities. I've done a lot of that sort of thing.*

GORDON: *Not at gunpoint, though.*

REG: *That was a first. I got in the car, and there was a gun in my face. That was the last thing I saw before they blindfolded me. Then they tied my hands and my feet behind me and tossed me in the trunk of the car and took me to a house just five miles from where Larry Flynnt got shot. They held me there for a while, and then it was back in the trunk of the car for fifty hours.*

PAUL: *They kept you in the trunk all the time?*

REG: *I now have a terrible case of claustrophobia.*

PAT: *It's a very curious thing. Reg had just been taking yoga. That probably permitted him to live through this experience.*

JOAN: *Really! What position did you assume?*

REG: *The cobra. That's a very relaxed position. And Pat's right. If you're mind has been conditioned, you respond better. And I had conditioned my mind through yoga by assuming these relatively uncomfortable positions and holding them for a period of time while learning to relax and to breathe. It's as if somebody or something told me to learn to do that 'cause it would come in handy.*

JANET: *But if you are not prepared in that way, what do you do?*

REG: *Basically, you try to stay calm.*

MARCIA: *But weren't you afraid for your life?*

REG: *You bet! But you have to try to dominate the environment, no matter what the handicaps are.*

GORDON: *How did you do that?*

REG: *By inventing one story and one joke and one line after another. You keep talking. You find every device that you can think of to engage people in conversation, and you try to keep the situation calm and cool. You try to defang the people who have* captured you. Talking is the key. And getting them to talk.

JULIA: *That's interesting. Back in the 60's, when the kids were getting stones thrown at them and getting clobbered by the rednecks and the cops too down in Mississippi, that's what Andy Young kept advising: Don't ever let any time go by without trying to talk and trying to talk and trying to talk. He said, "Don't let the cops stand twelve feet away from you. Go up to them and say something, any dumb thing. Make a dumb joke."*

REG: *That's dominating the environment. Andy was good at it. Better than Martin Luther King.*

JULIA: *Yes, Andy Young was superb. And he's the most decent human being I've ever met.*

CLAUDE: *How would you characterize the men who kidnapped you? Were they Southern redneck types?*

REG: *Yes. Very, very negative. But with backgrounds much like my own. They grew up in a small Southern town. Parents—lower middle class. That's my background. They had very limited educations but strong philosophical beliefs. That's why they chose me to kidnap. They wanted publicity for their rightwing cause.*

MARCIA: *Oh, they did? I thought they only wanted money.*

REG: *Money too.*

JANET: *How much money?*

REG: *$700,000.*

JANET: *That's a lot of money.*

REG: *It is. But it was the publicity that complicated the negotiations while I was in the trunk of the car, and that has caused all the controversy and litigation since then. The case is still in the courts. There was a hearing yesterday.*

PAUL: *After all this time?*

REG: *Now they want me convicted of perjury because I was misquoted.*

MARCIA: *But you were the victim. The victim ends up being the criminal?*

PAUL: *It's happened before.*

JULIA: *It happens in rape cases all the time. The victim is put on trial.*

GORDON: *What I don't understand how did you talk to your captors? How did you negotiate with them while you were in the trunk of the car?*

REG: *It wasn't easy. Just necessary. I don't recommend it.*

PAUL: *Didn't the* Examiner *have to be in on the negotiations? How did you manage that?*

REG: *That was ironic. A twist of fate. You see, the people who had taken Patty Hearst said that we would be the newspaper they would contact about returning her. So we set up a telephone and a 24hour telephone watch, expecting that call.*

GORDON: *So it was all in place.*

REG: *Yeah, all in place. But it was a complicated kind of negotiations that went on and on. You know, always those people have specific ideas about how they're going to accomplish everything, up to taking the money and releasing the hostage. But they don't know how to do that because that's an appointment with the police, when they go to pick up the dollars. And it inevitably ends up being a sort of a trap that they have created for themselves, and they can't get out of it. So if you can just stay alive until they walk into that trap. That has to be your goal.*

PAT: *When you hear of people being kidnapped, are you tempted to pick up the phone and call the family? Tell them not to panic and give them some idea of what they ought to do and shouldn't do?*

REG: No. I'll lecture or give a seminar if I'm asked. And sometimes people contact me. But I don't contact them. I think the intrusion that I would amount to in their lives would outweigh any possible value I would have to them. And I think that most people believe that they can handle the situation, and they are almost invariably right.

MARCIA: What about the police? How helpful are they in a kidnapping case?

REG: They're very good. They get maligned a lot, but in fact, they're good. And the FBI does a superb job.

CLAUDE: Are you worried now that it might happen again? Do you look over your shoulder when you go out?

REG: No. I don't think about it. If you let it get to you, you destroy yourself.

PAT: There are so many people here at the table who would be targets for this sort of thing, I should think. Gordon, with your name, you certainly would be.

GORDON: Yes. We hire guards during the night hours outside.

PAT: How about with when you were growing up? Did your family watch you? Where your activities curtailed because of this danger?

GORDON: No. In those days, there weren't kidnappings. I think the Lindbergh baby was the only case.

MARCIA: Joan's a target. I get letters at the station. Some weirdo is after her, and he's not keeping it a secret.

JOAN: That's been going on for 12 years. I've given the police a chance to handle it my way. They are supposed to be protecting the peace. I started with the Woodside Patrol. They don't carry *guns. I told them, "I don't want this person hurt or arrested. I want you to talk to him." But it is really hard to find a policeman who can relate to what I am talking about. I finally found one policeman in San Mateo who really understands. We have hashed it out for hours.*

MARCIA: *I have somebody after me right now. He is totally crazy. He's been in the state hospital in Napa, and the police have a record on him. But they say I have to press charges before they can do anything. I have no charges to press, but he calls me constantly and writes me letters and stands outside watching me.*

PAT: *Does he threaten you?*

MARCIA: *He threatens to love me.*

JULIA: *Have you talked to him, Marcia?*

MARCIA: *I did talk to him. I told him that I knew he was lonely because he had written about his loneliness in his letters. But that I couldn't do anything about that. Not because he wasn't a nice person, but because I was happily married. But that was a mistake. It encouraged him. He tried harder.*

JOAN: *It isn't always a mistake. I've had to deal with a lot of very unstable people with a big part of their lives missing. They have these fantasies they think I can fulfill. One boy, for instance, he was on booze and every kind of drug possible. I sat him down and said, "As long as you don't talk crazy, I'll talk to you." But he couldn't concentrate for more than five minutes. Then he would start talking gibberish again. Then he started acting crazy. He broke into the house. So I took him down to the highway and told him to leave and not to bother my life anymore. With him and a couple of others that direct confrontation has worked.*

JULIA: *Have there been times it didn't work?*

JOAN: *Oh, yes! There was one woman what was incredible. She* wanted to be part of the family. She was going to move in and cook dinners for Dave and me. She hung around and wouldn't go away. Everybody talked to her, and it didn't do a bit of good. So finally I went out and talked to her. I was severe. I was nasty. And the next day, she left a note on the gate saying it was so thrilling finally to see me. So when she came again, I called the police. That did it. These people are usually scared of the cops. When the cops arrive, they just kind of physically wither away.

CLAUDE: *The cop is the authority figure.*

JULIA: *Yes. I think that's true.*

PAT: *And with what I'm hearing is that these people are lonely and haven't learned how to handle the loneliness. We all have that in common, don't you think? Most everybody is lonely, even those who are constantly surrounded by people. You're constantly surrounded by people, Janet.*

JANET: *In politics there are many friendly faces and very few friends.*

PAT: *That is very well said.*

JANET: *I think you have to have a circle of friends. Regardless of what you're doing, you need support from friends.*

VILMA: *I don't think so. I don't think you have to have a circle of friends.*

JULIA: *You mean to be in politics, or what?*

VILMA: *No, for support. I think there are a lot of people in this world who don't have the talent for making friends.*

MARCIA: *But don't you think they're very lonely as a result?*

VILMA: *I'm not lonely.*

JOAN: *Don't you have any friends?*

VILMA: *No.*

PAT: *But we're your friends.*

VILMA: *Okay. Then I have friends.*

JOAN: *Do you prefer it this way? I mean do you prefer not to have a circle of intimate people?*

VILMA: *That's what I prefer, yes.*

CLAUDE: *But you know, that's very curious. You're terribly likable. You're very, very likable. But when you attack, you get everybody all lathered up. When you attacked the mayor, everybody jumped to her defense. And when you attacked the stand the newspaper took on a couple of issues, I bristled even though I'd more naturally be on your side.*

VILMA: *That's what I wanted to find out. Who would defend whom?*

CLAUDE: *But I didn't want to defend a lousy newspaper. Excuse me, Reg, relatively lousy.*

REG: *And do you think I was going to sit here and defend myself against an Archbishop Quinn piece when we've run a hundred pieces on the other side of that issue? I don't need that. You may need it, but I don't need it.*

VILMA: *I can understand that.*

CLAUDE: *But I'm your friend. I want to be your friend, Vilma.*

VILMA: *I want you to be.*

Vilma looked around the table. "I want all of you for friends," she said. It was Warm Fuzzy time again. In less than an hour, we had progressed from the horror of kidnapping through loneliness to friendship. It was a comfortable place to settle.

CHAPTER ELEVEN

1977

The Main Course Was Violence

It was a typical San Francisco day, fog rolling in over the water, licking at the bridge and city. I stood watching it, waiting for my guests. Ordinarily, I eagerly anticipate a Roundtable luncheon, but this day I was apprehensive. Not about the food or the table. I had tasted the food and knew that Gerri, the chef, had outdone herself. And if the day looked chill and forbidding outside, it was warm and spring-like within, the bright colors of tulips in a basket in the center of the table reflecting the pattern of the tablecloth.

No, I was apprehensive because of the strange, catastrophic events that had occurred in the lives of two of my guests. One was Daphne Greene, a theologian, proper wife and mother, upstanding citizen, recently indicted for kidnapping her own daughter. The other was gentle Father Miles Riley, who had just recovered from wounds inflicted by muggers. Also on the guest list this day was Eldridge Cleaver, who had once been a mugger himself. I wondered how he and a mugging victim would interact and thought, "The main course today will be violence." But then, of course, Eldridge Cleaver might not show. He had accepted two previous invitations and was yet to appear at a luncheon.

But this noon he was the first to arrive, carrying a camera. I was startled at his size, in sharp contrast to diminutive Merla Zellerbach, who came in immediately afterward. I had never met Eldridge Cleaver before, and I expected a voice and manner to match his stature. Instead, he asked softly and rather timidly, I

thought, if he could take our pictures. So that when Sidney Goldstein arrived with her camera, she could take a picture of Eldridge
taking pictures. Both were ready with cameras when Daphne
Greene limped in on crutches, mutely testifying that ski slopes
can be treacherous in spring.

Everybody arrived promptly that day, which doesn't always
happen at a Roundtable. And everybody wanted to hear, at once,

---

GUESTS

Eldridge Cleaver • Former Black militant; arrested in
1969, he skipped bail and fled the country, returning in
1975

Daphne Greene • Theologian and anti-Moonie fighter;
charged with kidnapping her daughter

Dr. Rollo May • Training and supervisory analyst at
the William Alanson White Institute of Psychology,
Psychiatry, and Psychoanalysis. He has made pioneering
contributions with such works as *The Meaning of Anxiety,
Love and Will,* and *Man's Search for Himself.*

Father Miles Riley • Roman Catholic priest; mugging
victim

Dr. Mimi Silbert • Psychologist and co-president
of Delancey Street, a successful organization for the
rehabilitation of ex-convicts. Mimi also works with the
police department.

Merla Zellerbach • Columnist and author

Marcia Brandwynne • TV anchorwoman

Sydney Goldstein • Head of programming at College of
Marin and photographer

about the mugging Miles Riley had suffered. So while we sipped
our wine he told the story, the violence of which contrasted sharp-
ly with his soothing priest's voice.

FR. MILES: *Well, I had taped my show on Channel 5 in San
Francisco and got through about ten o'clock. The radio station
in the East Bay for which I do a program was having a party. So
I went over there. It was good to see the wives, and disc jockeys,
and management. I enjoyed myself. But as I was leaving, about
11:30, I thought I should go to the bathroom. So I did. There was
one right off the lobby of the hotel in which the party was held.
After I was in there, a man started talking to me on the side, you
know, sort of urinal-to-urinal. And another man whipped around
behind me with a blackjack or something and knocked me out.
I hit the floor and came to seconds later you know, right away
in a big pool of blood in this garish bathroom scene. It was very
Clockwork Orange. I wasn't supposed to come to, I guess. The
one man kept smashing me, and both were screaming at me, like
"Why don't you stay knocked out?" and "Shut up" and "Don't
move." The screaming brought a bellhop to the door, and one of
the guys told him, "It's okay. He's just drunk. We are taking care
of him." I had been scared all along, but now I was really scared.
Afraid for my life. My attackers had conned my potential helper. I
begged them not to kill me, in a little child's voice. My eyes were
filled with blood. I couldn't see. But I heard everything. I heard
the bellhop or somebody open the door again. I raised my voice
as much as I could and called, "Help me! Please, help me!" My
attackers left in fright and my rescuers ministered to me and called
the police to take me to the hospital. And the first phrase that
began reverberating in my consciousness was, "Father, forgive
them. They don't know what they're doing." You know, as Jesus
hung on the cross, he didn't say, "We gotta change the institution"
or "We gotta get rid of these Roman oppressors" or "We gotta
get rid of these Jewish phonies." He said, "Father, forgive them."*

And that phrase kept coming back. It stuck with me as the police and the security guards questioned me. Yeah, would you believe it? The hotel had three security guards who had managed to miss the whole show. So that was in the back of my mind, this concept of forgiveness. Now I've been mugged before. I worked at San Quentin as chaplain for four years. I've dealt with the police for fifteen years as a Catholic priest, mostly a parish priest. I have been supportive of the police. I want to be supportive. But this is what I felt I had to say to them. What I did say to them. I said, "Gentlemen, I'm with you. You do your job, and I'll back you. But I don't think it's effective, this system. I do not want to cooperate with the system. I do not want to identify my attackers. I am going to try to reach them with forgiveness because I think it is more startling and possibly more effective." Then I called the newspapers and the TV and radio stations and asked them not to say anything, to let me say what I wanted to say on my own show. They all honored my request. I didn't realize I had that power or that they had that graciousness.

MERLA: *Could you have identified the muggers?*

FR. MILES: *I doubt it. The whole thing was too traumatic. I was too dazed. And my eyes were filled with blood the whole time. But most people that I thought I should try. My brothers and my dad thought I should try.*

Rollo May shook his gray mane. Mimi Silbert scowled slightly. Everybody had finished their drinks, and the soup had been served. It was a delicious, creamy asparagus soup, but for a while it went untasted. That frequently happens at the Roundtable. Food is ignored in favor of talk.

ROLLO MAY: *I think you are right, Miles.*

FR. MILES: *After the attack, my head was swollen and there were stitches. And I wore an eye patch. And everybody asked me about* *what had happened. The same three questions in the same order: Where did it happen? Did I have my collar on—that is, was I visibly a priest? And what color were the assailants? That was the fifth time I'd been mugged in fifteen years as a priest, and the other four times were in the church or in the priests' house, so what difference?*

DR. ROLLO: *You are definitely right, Miles. The present system does not work. In New York they mug a dozen times an hour. All my friends have been mugged. Reporting these people, incarcerating them. I don't see that this does very much good. There has to be some new system. What it is going to be is your faith against my guess. But it won't consist of can you identify them and then, if you can, let's put them in jail. You see, the more cops you have on a given beat, the more crime you have on that beat.*

DR. MIMI: *I don't agree with that.*

DR. ROLLO: *No? But it's factual.*

Mimi Silbert wanted to speak. She knew this subject well. Mimi works with John Maher at Delancey Street, a powerful organization for ex-cons, run by ex-cons. A slip of a woman, not five feet tall, Mimi had once stood her ground against a burly ex-drug addict and criminal. "You must never let them know you are afraid," she said afterward. And then admitted, "But when that encounter was over, my knees were like rubber!"

PAT: *What do you think of all this, Mimi?*

DR. MIMI: *I think there is no question that the system doesn't work, but essentially to have no system leaves the worst of people to keep ferreting among themselves. They go with the worst in themselves until something or someone forces them to take a real look at what they have done. I don't think they would understand what you did, Miles, forgiveness. I think it is important that you* *did it because otherwise you would have lived with bitterness and frustration and vengeance. But for them to change for most of us something has to jar us. Whether we hit rock bottom or bump into something enlightening. It is usually a bump.*

MERLA: *Like, the definition of a liberal is a conservative who has never been mugged. Everybody laughed, glad to have a release of tension. Miles was still smiling when he spoke.*

FR. MILES: *I think the "bump" is forgiveness. I think that's the place of departure.*

SYDNEY: *Oh, they don't know about your forgiveness. I think that's a blind spot with you, Miles.*

DR. MIMI: *Your forgiveness is meaningless and fake for them, Miles. They have to forgive themselves.*

All this time, Eldridge Cleaver was intensely focused on the conversation, his eyebrows lifting one at a time as he looked from speaker to speaker. I thought his point of view would be enlightening. I had only to say his name and he began talking.

ELDRIDGE: *I've mugged people in my life, amongst other things. I committed burglaries and armed robberies, and I never felt guilty. When I got away, it was just great. I just really enjoyed it.*

PAT: *And if someone has said, as Miles did, "Forgive him, he knows not what he's doing"?*

ELDRIDGE: *I would find that guy and rob him again. It has to do with the perception of the robber whether he feels justified in doing what he has done. The only time I ever did anything that I felt guilty about was rape. And I didn't get caught for it. But it was just*

> *I committed burglaries and armed robberies, and I never felt guilty.*

something that just ate me up.

MERLA: *What was your motivation for rape?*

ELDRIDGE: *I still have difficulty in ironing that out. The way it happened the first time, I was living with a girl in an apartment in Los Angeles, and we had to spend a couple of days in a motel while the apartment was painted. Well, we were sitting in the car outside this motel, waiting for our room to come up, and the girl with me saw her next door neighbor, who was a married man, going into this motel with a girl who wasn't his wife. She called to him, and he came over to the car and pleaded with her not to tell anybody. And I just had a big flash on the vulnerability of people who go to motels. There is a whole scene that's going on that can't be reported, nine times out of ten. I was on parole, and I had been selling marijuana, and I had this big wad of money on me. If somebody had robbed me, I couldn't have done anything. So, anyway, the next weekend I found myself back at the same motel.*

SYDNEY: *Why?*

ELDRIDGE: *Because I saw that these people could be ripped off with impunity. So I went back to do it. I followed a couple into a motel room, and I tied the guy up and put him in a closet and did what he had come there to do. And it wasn't reported. There is something about the motel situation that intrigued me, pulled me. I wrote a poem about motels. To me, a motel was like an obscene institution, you know? I kept going back, every weekend, to that motel and others. But years later, when I was in San Quentin, and then thereafter, it just ate me up because there was no way I could justify what I had done. It just kept coming back to me as something wrong. No problem with robbing a Safeway store, which I had also done. I was glad about that, you know. But this particular act, rape, it just drove me up the wall.*

Marcia Brandwynne fixed him with her large black eyes. Hers was a reporter's curiosity.

MARCIA: *But when you did these things when criminals rape and rob aren't they afraid of getting caught, of being put in jail, of their freedom being taken away?*

DR. MIMI: *Most of the people going around committing crimes really have no freedom to lose.*

ELDRIDGE: *You don't calculate that far. The act itself is what you want to accomplish. Most criminals don't really plan their retreat, you know? Like, how to get out of the bank after you get the money and the cops are coming. The guy may feel that if he didn't get killed, he got off lightly, you know? And you have to distinguish between crimes against property and crimes against the person.*

ROLLO MAY: *That's what rape is.*

ELDRIDGE: *If a guy goes after property, there's sort of a coldblooded calculation involved. He's weighed the risk, and he's weighed the gains, even to the extent of saying, "If I get this money and get away with it, great. But if I get caught..." Then he calculates the number of hours that he will spend in jail. And often they equate with the number of hours he would have had to work for the same amount. I used to do it all the time.*

DR. MIMI: *And it's better in jail almost, than some of the jobs.*

FR. MILES: *Plus, it's a crapshoot. You still have a chance of getting off Scotfree.*

SYDNEY: *I think this about life: that everyone wants to feel a sense of power over their lives and a sense of control, and most people don't. Committing crimes is a temporary surge of power. Rape certainly is. And research on this shows that women who become extremely aggressive rather than being the victim, who begin to take sexual initiative, then—*

... everyone wants to feel a sense of power over their lives and a sense of control, and most people don't.

DR. MIMI: *The rapist wilts and goes away?*

MERLA: *I've wondered about that. What would happen if you say, "This is fabulous! Where have you been all my life?"*

PAT: *It would be a very unusual woman who could do that.*

MARCIA: *If anybody could have done that, it would be Carolyn Craven. But she said she couldn't do it when it happened to her because she felt if the man could rape, he could kill.*

MERLA: *And also he kept saying, "Pretend you enjoy it," which is kind of weird.*

DR. MAY: *Who said this, the rapist?*

MARCIA: *Yes, this guy has committed seventy known rapes in Berkley. And just happened to hit on a reporter, Carolyn Craven of Channel 9.*

FR. MILES: *She was really gutsy.*

ELDRIDGE: *Do you think he chose her? Or was it random?*

MARCIA: *He doesn't know who the women are, but he watches their pattern for about five days and knows how they live. He has never chosen a house with a dog in it. Or a house with a husband or a male who is there regularly. It's always a woman alone or a woman with a child.*

DR. MAY: *He's still at large.*

PAT: *Yes. It's been headlined in the papers. Rollo doesn't watch TV or read the papers.*

DR. MAY: *Only the New York Times.*

ELDRIDGE: *I just want to point out something I am more and more impressed with as time goes by. That is, we have become more and more preoccupied with the penal code and the civil code. But there are other codes that really preceded these two. These are codes that are not policed by policemen but by family and community and self. And if we have a society that depends solely on the penal code and the policeman, then everything is already lost.*

MERLA: *You're right.*

ELDRIDGE: *It's really the policeman of the heart—*

The table was suddenly silent as people thought about this. Then they turned their attention to the chicken dish that had just been served. When the conversation resumed, it was in a lighter vein. Eldridge had recently been involved in designing men's clothing. Which reminded Mimi that when she was getting her Ph.D. in psychology, she had done a piece of research to determine whether men who wore jockey shorts or men who wore boxer shorts were more authoritarian. It turned out that authoritarian types wore boxer shorts. Conversation at the Roundtable isn't always solemn.

But Daphne Greene looked solemn. And she had been quiet, which was unlike her. She has a reputation as an active, energetic woman in conversation or sports. She'd been through a lot recently and I wondered if she would talk about it

PAT: *Daphne, some people here may not know about your experiences with your daughter. Would you mind telling us about it?*

DAPHNE: *I've been thinking about it as I listened to everybody talk. You know, for two years I was very outspoken against the parents who kidnapped their children away from religious organizations. I don't like the word "cult." I never have. And yet, we came to a position, after spending a weekend with our twenty-one-year old, of kidnapping her. So here I was someone firmly* *against a certain kind of behavior and then within one week, I was a criminal, arrested for kidnapping. And we did kidnap her. We did it in a very violent way. We blindfolded her. We put her in a van. We transported her someplace else. We kept her in a locked room. We, you know it was heavy-duty stuff. But it was not done the way the press puts it when they say, "Mrs. Green is a violent Moonhater." I don't feel that I am. But I do feel that everybody has a right to human dignity. They may not have a right to much else. But as soon as I see someone's dignity being stepped on, then it's time to do something. So we did it. We kidnapped her. That was the motivation. To restore dignity. And in the process, I lost my naiveté. And I hate that. It's really a beautiful thing to have.*

SYDNEY: *While you have it, it's a beautiful thing. But for millions of people struggling to survive, naiveté is a real luxury.*

DR. MIMI: *Exactly. If you have to survive in a mean, vicious world, you lose your naiveté before you're five years old.*

ELDRIDGE: *I wonder about your use of the word, Daphne.*

DAPHNE: *I think of somebody naive as being someone who doesn't believe in reality. But now I know reality. I know that the United States Government has the evidence they need to expose an organization that should be exposed, and I also know that they are being paid off not to do it. I know all this crap, and I've become cynical. I'm just now learning what Eldridge must have learned when he was ten: that there is a world of injustice.*

SYDNEY: *That the good guys are not necessarily the identified good guys. You could afford to believe in a just world when you and your family weren't affected. You didn't have to be cynical.*

DR. MIMI: *But the choice is not to become cynical! If the system needs changing, we will change it. Daphne, people like us are glad when people like you begin to realize that the world is unjust because then we will fight together to change it.*

ELDRIDGE: *For some reason the Moonies have been trying to develop a relationship. They've wanted to undertake some joint activities in the community with my group and their organization. And I've talked to them about debriefing and about their constitutional rights. I don't support their beliefs, but I support their rights under the Constitution. Anyway, I found this very interesting, what you had to say, Daphne. I'd only heard their side. You're the first concerned parent I've met.*

DAPHNE: *Rollo's had experiences with them, too. They would like to use his name.*

DR. MAY: *Every conference that they have, they invite me. I've refused every one of them and have even campaigned against them. But, ah, they are indefatigable.*

PAT: *Do they pay people?*

DR. MAY: *Oh, do they pay people! $3,000 plus all of your expenses for a day. That's a hell of a lot of money.*

MARCIA: *Those kids pull in four and five hundred dollars a day. Every one of them.*

FR. MILES: *I got sucked in, and I went for it. They sounded good and they looked good. They were talking Jesustalk. There are about a half-a-dozen pseudo-religious groups all over the country that are doing the same thing. And two things bother me about them. They're highly manipulative. And I think that's one of the greatest sins we can perpetrate on one another: to manipulate; to use other human beings. And, secondly, they're doing it in the name of religion. I think that is very unfair to all of us Muslims, Christians, Jews; everybody who is trying to get society back in touch with spiritual values. And we much need spiritual values at this particular time in history.*

CHAPTER TWELVE

1977

Of Joy and Sorrow

Busy people were sitting at my table this cold, wet day, and I knew they would soon be consulting their watches and dashing off. I wanted to ask The Question before that happened because today's question was, for me, an important one. It was also in two parts, so it would take longer than usual to answer. I wanted to know from each guest what had been his or her unhappiest experience that had become a growing experience, and what did each remember as the happiest time? I called on Father Miles Riley first because I knew I could count on him to set exactly the right tone. Father Miles, a handsome man with a top-of-the-line openness and an endearing sense of humor, leaned back in his chair to answer.

FR. MILES: *The unhappiest is easy. It's rejection. It's always been rejection. When I was a child, I competed with my mother for my father's affection, and with my six brothers and sisters for my parents' attention, with my peers for athletic and musical awards and academic honors. Life for me was one big competition. But the thing that hurt the most wasn't losing, although that hurt a lot. It was being ignored. Being "ditched," we used to call it. So to avoid that, to keep from being rejected, I followed other people's scripts. I lived my life to please them. They had control. I was successful, or not, according to their standards. I was important if they told me I was. If they rejected me, I was unworthy. As an adult this left me with a tremendous inadequacy. I was incapable*

*of intimacy. I was scared to death to be vulnerable. I give love
to everybody, but I could not be loved. I refused to be loved. I
was a compulsive helper, but no one could help me. Of course
by helping, I assured myself that I was needed. Then I was
hospitalized, and I had to think this all out, change my whole
vision of life. Life isn't the great competition. It isn't a huge game.
I finally saw it for what it is, a mysterious gift from God. And
the gift is mine to live. Mine alone. And I realized that when you
come to the end of your life, when you're dying, you experience
and appreciate some of the feelings that the person that I follow,
Jesus Christ, had and felt and expressed: That you are alone. It's
you. It's your soul. So I had to take responsibility for this precious*

GUESTS

Alex Hayley • Author of *Roots*

Jim Dunbar • Talk show host and radio program director

Father Miles Riley • A San Francisco-based reverend

Denise Minelli Hale • Hollywood socialite

David Sheff • Author of the book *Beautiful Boy*, now
adapted into an award-winning film

Ginetta Sagan • Founder of Amnesty International

Joan Brann • Director of the San Francisco Department
of State Reception Center

Marcia Brandwynne • T.V Anchor

Ailieen Hernandez • Urban consultant; second president
of N.O.W.

Bill Graham • Rock Impresario, owned Fillmore Records

gift of life and live it in and with the community. Remembering that Jesus said "Our father" when he taught us how to pray. He didn't say, "My father." We do need each other. We need to love and be loved, to helped and be helped. I can accept that now, and now my happiest moments don't come from winning or from other people's attentions. They come from being at peace. A deep peace within. I may not be happy on the outside, but I feel together. I feel right. I feel in touch with my roots. This has allowed me to accept my parents. I rejected them once ran away from home. They're multimillionaires with an 88-room house and a nine-hole golf course in the backyard. I couldn't handle that. I wanted no part of it, but now I can go home again. I've spent a good part of the past two years going home and learning who they are and falling in love with them. That's been my happiness.

DENISE: *That's very powerful.*

PAT: *Thanks, Miles. Hey, Jim Dunbar my roommate at KGO TV, what is your answer to* <u>The Question</u>?

JIM: *Well, I've probably had unhappier moments in the past, but I'll tell you about one that happened recently that really had me strung out. And that was a relationship that I thought was disintegrating with my son, who was coming into his young manhood. It had become very important that he begin to snap off some of his ties to me. And though I understood this, it was a very trying time. And I'm not terribly proud of the way I handled some of it. I made it difficult for him. I challenged him in a lot of ways that are upsetting to recall now. Because what it all amounted to, of course, was the fundamental struggle of a young man beginning to feel the need to assert his individuality and step out without the old man constantly underpinning him and catching him when he falls. I found it difficult to withdraw from that and let him fall on his butt a couple of times to learn that it doesn't hurt all that much. You don't die, you get up and try again. Well, I've just learned those things myself. The other side of all this is that the relationship has* turned around now. I began to let go and give him the opportunity to manage his own affairs. But I had anxiety about whether I had given him enough that he could measure up to the challenge out there. When you look at that, it's self-appraisal. It was myself I was doubting. Not him. And when I began to turn that loose and not let it run me so much, then I became aware of the wonderful things in this kid. Wonderful things.

ALEX: How old is he, Jim?

JIM DUNBAR: He's seventeen, eighteen on Friday. And he chose not to enter college this fall. He wanted to go back to Washington and work. I had a terrible struggle with that. He secured an admission, got a deferral, the whole thing. And I responded kind of outrageously. I was trapped in conventional expectations. You are seventeen and you are going to college. That's what you do when you're seventeen. It got to be a contest of wills. But with a lot of help from my wife and others and a lot of understanding from him, I was finally able to see that it was his life. So I gave up, and he has pursued this goal of his. And he is very fulfilled by it, much nurtured. And it has been a great source of pleasure and a real pride for me. It gives me a great deal of happiness now.

ALEX: I champion him. If I had my druthers, a kid ought to finish high school, go out and do a year in this world, and then go to college if he wants to.

JIM: I agree with that now, Alex. But I had to work through to it.

JIM: You were my son's age. I see what I risked.

PAT: Alex, are you going to answer _The Question_ now?

ALEX: No, I haven't thought of how I'll answer _The Question_. But I do have an anecdote because what Jim said reminded me of my father. I think from the day I was born, he was determined that I was going to get a Ph.D. He had a Master's degree, so the children were gonna do better. I was equally determined I wasn't *going to get a Ph.D. From the day I was old enough to know what that was. Well, when my dad was at Cornell, he had joined some fraternity and every Sunday when he dressed for church, he wore a vest and a very fine chain on which hung this fraternity key. After church he would always hold court in the churchyard, and people would gather 'round and listen to him because he was so wise. And while he talked, he would swing this little key. It hypnotized his audience. Except for Scrap Green. One Sunday she asked, "'Fessor Hayley, what is that thing?" That was all he needed. He launched into an erudite explanation that included much Latin and Greek, and of course nobody understood a word. And when he was through, Scrap asked him, "but 'Fessor Hayley, what do that key open?"*

AILEEN: *What a profound question! Real food for thought.*

PAT: *Aileen?*

AILEEN: *Pat, I'll have a go at* The Question. *It's hard for me to answer because I don't tend to think of the happiest or the saddest moment. But perhaps the saddest was my arrival in Washington, D.C. in 1943. And I discovered then that the capital of the United States was totally segregated, which I hadn't known until I got there. And I think that had a lot to do with what became the focus of my life. And I think my happiest experience is even simpler than that. At 51 I discovered my parents as friends. So in the past three or four years, I have had such a close friendship with my mother and father. I've discovered them to be marvelous human beings. I'm so glad they've lived this long, otherwise I might have missed their friendship. I would have had only a memory of my mother and father as authority figures telling me what to do.*

PAT: *I envy that experience, Aileen. Alex, are you ready yet?*

ALEX: *Not yet.*

PAT: *Then Denise, it's your turn, darlin'.*

DENISE: *I never cry. It's not in my nature. But I'm on the verge, just from thinking of the sorrows and the joys.*

PAT: *Please continue, Denise, you have a rapt audience.*

DENISE: *I was born in Belgrade. Very well born. I was the first child and the first grandchild. Very spoiled. Everything was my way. Even when the Germans came, and the family was losing right and left, suffering, it was kept from me as much as possible. I still felt secure, even when I was hurting because my grandfather was always there to make it right. He stood between the war and me. I depended on him for that. I knew he would never let me down. Oh, I knew I would cry, remembering him.*

Denise started crying and Ginetta comforted her. Their backgrounds were so similar. And all of us felt for her and with her. For a while the room was very still. Then Denise took a deep breath. She could talk again.

DENISE: *Then the Russians liberated us from the Germans, and my father said that was a good thing. But I was separated from my family from my father and my mother and my brothers and sisters everybody I loved. Especially my grandfather. I no longer had him to protect me. And I was in this rowboat with all these other children, headed for Italy.*

We suffered desperately. I was near death when we were, when we were finally picked up by an English captain. At first the boat wouldn't pick us up. They didn't want refugee children aboard. The disruption. The responsibility. But then they did pick us up. I guess I owe my life to the captain who made the decision. We still correspond. And last year he sent me a watercolor of the ship. But we couldn't stay on the ship forever. They had to take us some place. They took us to a displaced persons' camp. That's the place where you throw everybody that nobody wants, the garbage heap of humanity. I had never seen such people before. I found no one there strong, as my grandfather was strong. It was night. And that night, I guess, I grew up. I realized that I was on my own. No family to love me. No grandfather to protect me, to make everything all right. I will never forget that night.

GINETTA: *Now we won't either.*

PAT: *And now a happy time to share?*

DENISE: *Oh, yes. My wedding to my present husband. It wasn't my first wedding, so we couldn't marry in the church. But we had been looking forward to this moment through three years of problems and tragedies and finally we were standing there before the judge. And I began to cry. And, as I say, that's not my nature. But I was so happy. And when I started to cry, my husband started to cry too. And then everybody cried. It was a crying ceremony. Because there was such happiness.*

PAT: *Now we can remember your happiness as well as your troubles.*

ALEX: *I defer to you, Patsy Lou.*

PAT: *Well, okay. But what I'm going to say is very trivial compared to what we have been hearing. Still, it did happen to me. I came to San Francisco, and I made a nice life for myself, and I became well known, and I loved every minute of it. I really enjoyed reading in the paper that I was an outstanding hostess. It made me feel important. It validated me as a human being because I didn't have that much confidence in who I really was. Then I married Mel Belli, a former attorney. Now I'm going to cry. I had the marriage annulled. And it was in all the papers, magazines, and in tabloids, aired for everyone to gossip about. It absolutely devastated my self image. I was no longer that fine, outstanding person I used to read about in the press. Well, you see, Denise? I cry too. I want my guests to feel comfortable.*

ALEX: *I used to hold your towel back in those days, Pat.*

PAT: *Yes, you did. Alex did. He was so great about it. He helped me to see beyond the moment. But I think to have your self image destroyed is a devastating thing.*

DENISE: *You have to decide you're going to survive.*

PAT: *And I did. And there have been many happy times. I married Alfred. I became an author. And I got away from my images of myself that were false. I became somebody to myself. That's important.*

ALEX: *There are peaks only because there are valleys.*

JIM: *That's why Denise cries when she's happy and when she's sad. We all do.*

We needed a break from the intensity of our conversation; therefore I was happy that the cook arrived bearing a Cinnamon Apple Gateau, sure to be delicious. We took a collective breath and happily dug into the low fat cheese with honey and apples. This, coupled with fresh ground French Roast coffee supplied the energy for continuing our enlightening talk.

MARCIA: *Ah, now I feel like telling my stories.*

She paused to sip her coffee.

MARCIA: *Well, for my graduation from high school, I had received a ticket to California to visit my sister. So when my mother told me to get out, I packed my bags and got on a plane. I was so scared. But when the plane took off, I remembered myself sitting on 92nd Street and Broadway and wanting exactly this. So there was that excitement. I said, "This is it. This is freedom." And I never went back.*

> **I said, "This is it. This is freedom." And I never went back.**

GINETTA: *You've never gone back?*

I knew I had to start my life over. And I knew I was able to do that.

MARCIA: No, I've never gone back. I've come to terms with my family. But I came out here by myself. I've managed by myself. And I've never gone back.

PAT: Joan, we haven't heard from you.

JOAN: I don't have to think about an answer to your question. The saddest thing that happened to me was losing a son to the revolution that happened in the 1960s. He was seventeen too. I insisted that he go to the University of California. And he did and joined a revolutionary group. Now he is one of hijackers in Cuba. He can never, never come home. I had an opportunity in 1976 to go to Cuba and see him. And while I was there, my husband committed suicide. I came home utterly devastated. My husband was dead. I had to leave this child I hadn't seen for six years. And everything in my life had collapsed. Everything. There was no money. Because it was suicide, there was no insurance. There was just nothing. No one to lean on. No one to live for. My husband was Jewish, and we had the Psalms said, and I read those Psalms day and night until finally I knew what David meant. I gathered strength. It took a long time. But I lost my fear. I knew I had to start my life over. And I knew I was able to do that. That was probably the greatest thing that ever happened to me. So now when I meet people, no matter how great they are, I can look at each as just another human being. We reach pinnacles, and we fall, and we pick ourselves up again. And it happens to everybody. That understanding has been very helpful to me at the Reception Center. When everyone else was hysterical and wondering whether they should curtsy or what when the Prince of Wales visited, I thought, the poor guy is probably tired of all these shivering, shaking, uncertain people. So I just put out my and said, "How do you do." I don't find anybody overwhelming anymore. We're all human.

PAT: *Ginetta what's your answer to* <u>The Question</u>*?*

GINETTA: *I was suddenly alone. All my life I had spent my nights in a comfortable bed, but that night I slept in a deserted boarded up building. It was so cold. It was the most miserable night. And in the morning, I knew my parents had been taken. And that was the devastating thing. But I won't dwell on that. I want to go on to something that happened only last year. I've always admired people who had the courage to say "No!" To authority when authority was wrong. So I've always admired the German general who was ordered to blow up Paris and did not do it. That took a lot of courage. Last year I was in Detroit to speak about Amnesty International, and I was guest for the night in the home of a Unitarian minister whose family came from Austria, and the wife came from Germany. As we sat around the fireplace that evening, we were talking, and I mentioned that one of people I most admired was this General. At which point there was a dead silence. And then, the wife got up and kissed me. And she said, "He was my father."*

ALEX: *Oh, boy!*

GINETTA: *Later, when I was in Vienna, I met the family. And that was the nicest the nicest.*

PAT: *Ginetta, what a lovely memory! Bill, we haven't heard from you.*

BILL: *I was a displaced refugee. I came to the States when I was eleven. I wasn't adopted because nobody knew what had happened to my parents. So I was put in a foster home in the Bronx. This family had a boy who was two years older than I was. And the reason they took me into their home was that he was studying German and French in school, and those where the only two languages I spoke when I got here. Well, I got here in September of '41 and three months later, the war broke out between Germany and America. The kids didn't care what your*

religion was. *If you spoke German, you were a Nazi. So I got my
head kicked in going to and from school every day. I decided
there was nothing to do but learn English very quickly and speak
it without an accent. And sure enough, in six months I was the
only guy out of all the kids that came over on my boat who had
no accent because I didn't want to keep fighting every day. When
I came here, I weighed forty-three pounds, and I had rickets. I was
in bad shape. And my foster mother took care of me and fed me
and fed me. She was an amazing woman. But I didn't appreciate
her. I always accused her of not being fair to me because I wasn't
her child. I thought she favored my foster brother. I was always
accusing her of that. "You wouldn't yell at me if I was your son. He
gets the lean meat, and I get the meat with fat. He gets the middle
of the bread, and I get the end." It never stopped.*

*I wasn't a pleasant child. I was very arrogant, with a chip on
my shoulder. I became isolated and took to the streets. I played a
lot of ball, did some gambling, stole a couple of hubcaps. Not like
my foster brother. He was studious, close to the family, very, very
bright. Classically oriented. Loved ballet. I was into jazz and Latin
music. I chased the ladies. Finally, we were both drafted. He was
stationed in the States, and I was sent to Korea. While I was there,
the Red Cross sent a message that my foster mother was ill. But
the army geniuses decided that she wasn't that ill, so they didn't
grant me leave to go see her. Then another message reached
the front. My foster mother was worse. I was flown back to the
States, but I was too late. She had already passed away. When I
got home, my foster father was consumed with grief. He couldn't
stop crying. He said, "Why did she have to leave? She was only
forty three." And over and over he said, "And she took these two
unknowns into her bosom and made them her own." I tried to
remind him that I was the unknown and Roy was his real son, but
Roy took me into the other room and told me what I had never
known before: He wasn't their real son; he had been a doorstep
baby. And then I had this vision of the years and years I had torn*

into that woman, and my foster father, too, accusing them of favoring their real son. I felt such remorse. It was the low point of my life, the very lowest.

DENISE: *I may cry again.*

BILL: *Then I'll tell you about a high point in my life. My family had been split up since I was a child. Both parents and one sister went in the camps. Four sisters and I survived. But we were scattered all over the world in Israel, in Geneva, in Vienna, in San Francisco. We hadn't all been together since 1939. So in 1977, when I got my first substantial chunk of money, I rented a house in Seacliff for a month and sent for my sisters and brothers-in-law. Well, we hadn't been together twenty minutes when they were at each other, arguing, yelling, and screaming.*

PAT: *Bill, you're ruining the story!*

BILL: *You have to understand, I was the youngest and the only boy. To them, I was still two and a half years old. They were all quarreling about who would do what with me and for me.*

MARCIA: *Did they keep it up?*

BILL: *No. We found our common drink, which was vodka with a little lemon. But we had no common language because everybody had stopped speaking German over the years. We hated it because of the horrors we had been through. But together we were able to forget the horrors and remember the good times. So that night we sat together, very close to one another. And we spoke German, and we sang the old German folksongs. And that night has to be the high point in my life.*

PAT: *I should think so.*

ALFRED: *That would be a high point in any life.*

PAT: *Alex, are you going to volunteer to tell your story?*

ALEX: *I think not. You know, I deal in stories and anecdotes.*

They're my stock in trade. But I've been sitting here, listening, and I couldn't match any of the stories I've heard. I wouldn't try. They've been real and moving. I'm sure that we will all take away from this table a glow from what we have heard that will arm us for a long time, no matter how much it storms outside.

CHAPTER THIRTEEN

1977
Roots

A wild, winddriven rain was dashing against the windows, and a fire was crackling in the grate. The doorbell rang, and Alex Hayley came in, dripping wet, but radiant. He was carrying a flight bag.

"Alex! I'm so glad to see you," I exclaimed. "I was afraid maybe your plane wouldn't make it from Los Angeles in all this weather."

"Then I would have had to walk here in the rain, Patsy Lou." Alex, an old friend, always calls me by my childhood name.

I took his coat, but he kept the flight bag and warmed himself by the fire until other guests arrived. Then he emptied the flight bag on the dining table Twenty copies of *Roots*, each in a different language. We examined the translations as we sipped our wine. I asked Alex if fame had changed his life.

ALEX: *Yes. And I'm not used to it yet. I keep forgetting that I can't do anything privately anymore. I was in Washington, the other day, and realized that I was going to need a tuxedo, and I hadn't packed one. So I had to rent one. And while they were fitting the pants, I ran across the street for a pack of cigarettes. Within five minutes there were two hundred people in the store, each wanting an autograph. It took me by surprise. I feel awkward and kind of embarrassed in situations like that. Because I feel I'm pretty much as I always was, but other people react differently. It's also embarrassing to read in the press about my wife. The press keeps giving me a new one everywhere I go.*

PAT: *People are always saying to me "Alex got married, did you know?"*

ALEX: *And relatives. We all have relatives we don't know about. But now mine are popping up everywhere. Legions of them! They'll say their grandmother was somebody you know was your grandmother's sister, but you never heard of this person.*

PAT: *Writers frequently manage to remain fairly anonymous. Whereas someone in television or the movies is always recognized.*

ALEX: *I can attest to that. Everything was pretty quiet, even when Roots as a book was just running away. And then the television show played. And on the last night of the show, when 80 million people were watching, I came on for the last four minutes. That was all. But the next morning when I go to out of the cab at Kennedy Airport to catch the plane for Los Angeles, I was mobbed. Such a crowd, pushing, pulling and jostling. The airline people, the ones in the blazer jackets, had to rescue me. They got me into a room, and then they took me to the plane. So I learned for the first time that there's a way that they can put you on planes that isn't known about.*

ALFRED: *I don't think you'll ever go back to cooking again, Alex.*

ALEX: *No, but I can still cook. Just as you can still drive a truck.*

PAT: *Al is not going to do his truck driver act today!*

ALEX: *No, but Al knows he can drive a truck no matter what happens. And if this bubble bursts, I know I can cook. And I know I can get a job as a cook. That's a great security thing. I don't expect to do it, but the point is, I could do it.*

PAT: *I don't think they'd hire Al to drive a truck.*

DENISE: *Why not?*

PAT: *He doesn't belong to the union.*

AILEEN: *He's going to be a roofer.*

ALFRED: *Yes, Aileen called this morning and I said, "Who is it? Can I help you?" And she said, "My roof's leaking and I can't get a roofer."*

GUESTS

Denise Hale • International society figure. Denise is an enigma to many. Married to an enormously successful man, she has gained a great reputation as a hostess. I was curious to get below the surface and discover the real person.

Jim Dunbar • San Francisco radio and television host. He often plays the role of Devil's advocate. He is well spoken and genial. But one gets the feeling he is more comfortable in the role of host than that of guest.

Father Miles Riley • Roman Catholic priest. Father Miles is a sensitive, deeply caring person. He has a great sense of humor and laughs easily with others. Often I ask him questions first, as I know I will get a thoughtful, honest answer.

Alfred Wilsey • Successful businessman and my husband. My book, *The Intruders* is dedicated "to Alfred Wilsey, who saved my life and then made it worth living." His personality belies his looks, as a pixie quality lurks near the serious appearing surface.

Alex Hayley • Author of *Roots* and *The Autobiography of Malcolm X*. His warmth embraces you even at a distance. Alex speaks in a quietly melodic manner, accompanied by concise gestures. He is a captivating storyteller.

AILEEN: *Tell them what you said to me.*

ALFRED: *I said, "It's just because you're Black, that's all." And she said. "I hadn't thought about that. I thought it was because I'm a woman."*

AILEEN: *What he also said was that he'd be right over to fix my roof, which I thought was marvelous. Then I discovered everybody is having the same problem. Nobody can get a roofer right now.*

Joan Brann • Director of the San Francisco Department of State Reception Center. Joan is short, 5' 2" with a generous figure and a contained personality. One gets the feeling of quiet competency and a resilient nature.

Ginetta Sagan • Founder of Amnesty International, which received the 1977 Nobel Peace Prize. She is a small woman with a softly accented voice and a certain sweetness. When she speaks, everyone is very quiet in order not to miss a word.

Bill Graham • Rock impresario. When Bill enters a room, you know he's there. He has a vigorous nature and a thoughtful manner. When he talks, he often leans back in his chair and sprawls in comfort.

Marcia Brandwynne • Television anchorwoman. Marcia exudes goodwill and warmth. She is a favorite at the Roundtable, which she usually attends. Her vibrant personality is an invaluable aid in getting others to open up.

Aileen Hernandez • Urban consultant. Past national president of N.O.W. She is a stately, Black woman who speaks with great knowledge and dignity. She has often been asked to run for public office, but has so far declined.

So this kind of thing helps us to have a better understanding of your own paranoia.

I saw Ginetta Sagan and Jim Dunbar were carrying on a private conversation at one side of the table. Instead of ringing the bell, I decided to ask Ginetta a question. Ginetta is small and soft-spoken. She enunciates her words carefully, as do many people for whom English is a second language.

PAT: *Ginetta, it's such wonderful news about Amnesty International winning the Nobel peace prize. Would you tell us how you got involved in Amnesty International?*

GINETTA: *Well, during World War II, many people, just like some of you around this table, were in jail or deported or compelled to hide. Not just because they were Jewish, but also because they were supportive of freedom of expression.*

ALFRED: *This is in Italy?*

GINETTA: *This was in Italy. So I became a smuggler. Not of goods but of people. I had never done any such thing in my life, but you learn fast when the need arises. And I became involved in the underground. Eventually my luck ran out and I had a firsthand experience on the other side of the walls. After the war, people were still jailed for their political opinions, but I was disappointed that people who were willing to help political prisoners in communist countries were not willing to help political prisoners in other countries and vice versa. I felt that people who were not criminals should not be imprisoned. I began with a group that was helping individual prisoners in Spain, in Portugal, in the USSR, and Czechoslovakia. But it was a small, pitiful effort. So in 1961, when Amnesty International started, I liked the concept. The aim was to help all people, regardless of race, religion, color or political affiliation provided they had not used or advocated violence.*

*That point was important to me. So I joined. I was a member in
Washington, D.C., but when I came to San Francisco, I found that
nobody had ever heard of Amnesty International. So our start
here was small Fifty three members. We had to keep explaining
what we were about. Even when you invited us to speak on your
TV show, Jim, you didn't understand that we were trying to do, did
you? My feeling was that you expected us to talk about amnesty
for draft resisters. Do you remember that?*

JIM: *You got a lot of response from that exposure, didn't you?*

GINETTA: *Oh, yes. Always after we spoke, explaining what we
were doing, people came forward and joined. We now have seven
thousand members in the Bay Area, and sixty to seventy thousand
nationwide. But it's not easy to explain to the American people
that there are innocent people in jails. Mostly Americans think that
if someone is in jail, then that person has committed a crime. Even
when you explain that this journalist or judge or religious person
or peasant leader is in jail simply because they disagreed with the
policy of the government, the American will often find a logical
reason. They may argue that the country has so many economic
problems that they have to lock up critics in order to get the job
done, to bring the country to a better standard of living. Then I
have to point out that they're locking up the best brains that could
sit down with the government leaders and discuss what needs to
be done and, through a free exchange of ideas, perhaps come up
with better solutions.*

AILEEN: *Are there any political prisoners in this country?*

GINETTA: *Eighteen, at present.*

MARCIA: *Almost all Black?*

GINETTA: *Almost all Black. And all those that were adopted by
Amnesty International were Black. Two in Florida were condemned
for killing a white gas station owner. I am always most reluctant*

when it comes to criminal cases. But investigation showed it was quite possible that they had been condemned not for the crime but because they were Black. So they were adopted. In the case of a Black activist in Buffalo, New York, there was never any doubt. He sold mostly leftist literature, and the police made an agreement with a known criminal to suspend the criminal's sentence if the criminal would plant drugs in the leftist's store. That's what happened. But then the criminal had power of conscience and contacted us. So the chairman of Amnesty International spoke to the governor of New York, and the case was investigated, and the leftist is now free.

PAT: *Ginetta, has winning the Nobel Prize been helpful in your work?*

GINETTA: *Oh, yes! The telephone never stops ringing. But above all, I think, it will help break through the misconceptions people have had about Amnesty International. Some think the organization must be fascist because it helps people unjustly confined in the USSR or Eastern Europe or other communist countries. Or they think it is communist because it helps people in Chile, or Brazil of Indonesia. I believe the prize and the publicity has made it clear what we really are and what we're trying to do.*

PAT: *Denise, you were once behind walls, weren't you? In a concentration camp?*

DENISE: *I was a refugee. My country is Yugoslavia, and we are the troublemakers of the world, you know.*

ALFRED: *Just you?*

DENISE: *My mother asked me to send Mr. Hayley's book because we're in search of our roots too. That is very important to us. Even today I find myself asking people, "Are you Serb? Are you Croat?"*

ALEX: *Where is your mother?*

DENISE: *In Belgrade. My father, mother, the whole family is in Belgrade. We are Serbs.*

ALEX: *I'd love to send her a book. What language should it be?*

DENISE: *I have to send English because it hasn't been translated there. Ours is a Slavic language. We have the same alphabet as the Russian language. And we are Greek Orthodox. Then we have the Croats, who are Roman Catholic. In 1941, when the Germans took over, these invaders, the Germans and Croats, caught a million Serbs and killed them overnight. It's not the something to talk about at lunchtime.*

PAT: *We talk about everything at lunchtime here!*

DENISE: *There is an inbred hatred between Serb and Croat. The feelings run very deep. My mother's sister married Croat. The family did not talk to her for twenty years. It's very distressing. I don't think the problem will ever be solved. It continues. My father was put in jail for three or four years because he believed the Russians gave us freedom, what freedom we had. He was jailed for his opinion.*

ALFRED: *Do the Serbs and Croatians have common roots way back?*

DENISE: *No, no; I don't think so. We are Slavs and they came from somewhere somewhere else.*

Although we talk of many things, at the Roundtable, I could see that Denise was uncomfortable. Her face and voice had grown tense, and she was twisting a ring on her finger. She was obviously grappling with feelings that were painful for her. I thought she would prefer not to be the center of attention at the moment. I turned to Aileen Hernandez with a question far from the subject we had been discussing.

PAT: *Aileen, what did you think of the recent equal rights amendment conference in Houston?*

AILEEN: *Well, it's nice to think about it from three thousand miles away! It was like any big convention. The parades and the speeches and the panoply were the show. But what happens behind the scenes creates the impact. I've been trying to understand why it is that we have had so much trouble with the ERA. Because we have five hundred or six hundred national organizations not all of them women's organizations supporting the ERA. And there are maybe four or five organizations that aren't supporting the ERA. But what happens? If the proside says something, the media rushes out to get the anti-side to say something. So it's like five hundred to one, but the one gets a huge proportion of the coverage.*

JIM: *And then there is Phyllis Schlafly. She's just very effective. Excellent. A pro.*

AILEEN: *I give her credit for that. She's very articulate, but totally unprincipled. She does not mind lying. She does not mind telling people things that appeal to their worst fear so that they will be on her side.*

MARCIA: *How do people get chosen for these conferences, Aileen?*

AILEEN: *Well, that's part of the problem. The people who ran the state committees were chosen from Washington. And those doing the choosing in Washington didn't know the people at the state level. They were just trying to get nicely balanced committees. I don't think that's the way you should do it. I think if you're going to have a statewide conference, you open it up and invite everybody to come. You may have a total madhouse at first. But it's better to do that than to keep it so close to your vest that everybody suspects that you don't want participation. And that's what happened in this case.*

FR. MILES: *Aileen, I watched the conference on TV one night, and I was flabbergasted! Are there any really that many lesbians in the country who are that oppressed? Or is that two questions?*

AILEEN: *Well, I think if you are a lesbian, you are oppressed. Particularly in employment. I don't think there's any question that if somebody knows you're a homosexual, and you go to one of these nice, straight-laced corporations, you are not going to get hired. They probably won't say why, but the bottom line will be that you're not getting hired because you're a homosexual.*

ALFRED: *Do you think that's still true?*

AILEEN: *Yes. And the reason I say this, I deal with a lot of very straight-laced corporations in my training programs. And in these programs, people are always off the wall with side comments about homosexuals. They don't very much make snide remarks about minorities anymore because that's no longer polite. But homosexuals and women are still fair game for jokes. There's that very quick kind of giggle around the room. I've come away from these sessions thinking that many of the men in charge of corporations must feel threatened by the whole issue of sexuality.*

JIM: *The gay community, taken as a whole, is pretty productive—a creative, getting-on-with sort of group. There are a lot of employed gays these days. Ipso facto, what you're saying just ain't so anymore.*

PAT: *Perhaps they were hired before they came out of the closet.*

ALFRED: *I think that's it. No one knew when they were hired. And having got seniority or acceptance, then slowly it begins to come out that they are gay. I agree completely with Aileen. A gay person is subject to great prejudice.*

MARCIA: *But do you think women should be dealing with this particular issue?*

AILEEN: *Oh, I think it's fundamental. Because if you can split the* women's movement over the issue of lesbianism by saying some of you are okay and some of are not, then we're all in trouble again. The lesbian is the one with the real problem. When people talk of gay rights, they're usually talking about rights for gay men, not gay women. And when a woman, for whatever reason, chooses not to identify herself with a man, then she's called a lesbian, and that's supposed to be the worst thing you can call her. I think it's much as it was with the Jews in Germany. When they came to get the Jews, many who were not Jews put on the Jewish armband. When that happens you can't making an issue anymore. It becomes a non-issue. And that's what's happening in the women's movement with the lesbian issue.

MARCIA: Well, I'm concerned that it is diverting attention from my other important issues.

AILEEN: It seems to me it is focusing heavily on people's sexuality, which after all is a minor portion of their lives. I don't know why anybody would want to make the crucial issue that small portion of life dealing with what happens in private between them and another human being. But I respect their right to do it. I would defend it.

BILL: I would hire a gay person without any qualms. It never bothers me. I would be much more concerned with a women's libber. Because too many of the libbers that I've met want to make change for the sake of change. They want the force an issue.

AILEEN: The terminology "libber" today is offensive.

PAT: It's offensive to me too. Bill, you've just offended us.

AILEEN: This again points out that when some people are projected in a certain way, their coloration extends to the entire group. For example, a Black person in the United States and I think probably Joan and Alex will agree with me we Blacks are never free to be totally ourselves. If one of us says something people disagree with, it can be said that all Blacks think the same way.

DENISE: *How about asking us other minorities here?*

AILEEN: *Yes. For any minority, I think that's true. If the lesbian is seen as a threat to family life, you identify negatively with the whole women's movement.*

BILL: *I've been very lucky. So have a lot of other expatriates, not only here but elsewhere in London, Sweden. And a huge number of people involved in the entertainment world. We've made huge amounts of money. But how do you handle yourself when you've been fortunate enough to buy a 12-acre mountain in California? And all of a sudden, this kid from the Bronx pushes a button and his gate opens and that's my house! I don't think too many of us have used our opportunities well or learned how to utilize the power we have. I guess that's why I'm disenchanted. Actually, I started getting out in 1971 when I closed the two Fillmores on both coasts that had made a tremendous sum of money. But now, in 1977, is the first that I'm beginning to do something other than simonizing the success machine.*

ALEX: *Marvelous expression!*

BILL: *In several ways that I'd rather not talk about, I'm getting involved in the community. But one project that I would like to talk about has to do with the people from that special era, from about '65 to '75, who thought if we just watered the lawn and had these flowers come up and smoked those lovely cigarettes, everybody would be all right, including the Middle East. But, of course, it didn't happen that way. Well, we are all somewhere between 25 and 40 now All these people from that era. And we live in the capital of that fantasy society, California. And we have nowhere to go to meet each other. Nothing to do in our spare time but watch TV or go to a bar or get stoned at somebody's house. Years ago, when I first came here, when I was 24 or 25, there was a club, up in Fairfax. Friends took me there. We went swimming, played badminton, and volleyball. We met people and had dinner* *and went dancing and maybe picked up a lady. I'd like to create a place like that for public assemblage outdoors. Not a private club. Just for a few bucks. So that people can go there and meet other people and just enjoy themselves.*

PAT: *You've touched on something so important. That's really the reason I have my Roundtable. To reach out to people, to touch someone else's life and have them touch my life. And it didn't just happen. You have to make it happen.*

BILL: *I lived in Mill Valley for more than six years, and I am sorry to thank you that in all that time, I've never repeat, never met one neighbor. I'm ashamed of that.*

MARCIA: *I was raised on the streets of New York where you meet because if you have the ball, you start the game. And you do meet, and you make wonderful friendships. I still have friendships from Brooklyn, circa 1949.*

BILL: *Something I've noticed is that now you can drive around on Saturday and Sunday and nineteen out of twenty schoolyards are empty. In the old days in New York, if you didn't get up at eight o'clock and go down and claim the court*

MARCIA: *You didn't get a court. How about, "I Challenge!" I mean, those were the great words I Challenge! And you got to meet people.*

DENISE: *In Belgrade you knew everybody. My mother knew everybody for blocks around.*

BILL: *I think that part of the problem is that when you start to make it, then you have to devote yourself to that. You have to lube and oil all that. I maintain that success is much more difficult a challenge than failure.*

ALEX: *I'd agree.*

BILL: *I only know a couple in my business, for instance, who play*

*facilities smaller than they can get away with. If somebody can
sell ten thousand seats, then he wants to play a fifteen thousand
seater. And you say to them, "Hey, man, like five years ago when
you started you said to me that when you made it, you always
want to play in the small places where you could communicate
with people and feel their sweat. What happened to that?" And he
says, "Heyeyey! Don't bug me!" He's lost sight of who he was and
who he started out to become. You know? He's all wrapped up in
his success.*

"Joan, which of the America's we've been talking about today do
you show your official visitors?" I asked Joan Brann, who had been
listening but not talking. Joan had recently been appointed head
of the State Department Reception Center in San Francisco. In
the so-called enlightened 70's, the appointment of a Black woman
to this important post had been controversial. A controversy that
occupied the front pages of newspapers for quite a while. Through
it all Joan had quietly attended to her new duties, proving by her
demeanor that she was right for the job. Now she answered with a
vibrant, enthusiastic voice.

JOAN: *I feel I have a great responsibility in what I'm doing a
responsibility to show our guests the positive aspects of America.
And I can do that honestly. I've traveled a lot around the world, so
I can make comparisons. And this is a great country, with open,
friendly, warm people. Just the fact that I'm a Black woman in the
position I'm in tells them something positive about this country. I
don't want to sound syrupy, but I really love America even though
America won't allow me to be its true daughter, though that is
what I believe I am.*

DENISE: *Why do you say that America will not allow?*

JOAN: *Because I am Black. And if you are Black in America, you* are first Black, and then you are an American. You cannot be an American first, even though that is what, indeed, we are.

Until Mr. Hayley did it for us, we had no roots anywhere else. We don't speak any other language. We celebrate no other holidays. We have no foreign allegiance. We don't send money out of the country. We are solely, wholly Americans.

DENISE: What about the future? Or do you think it will always be this way?

JOAN: I think that America is the laboratory of the future where we are thrashing out these problems. I don't think that humanity is complete where it is. To me, we are evolving towards what can be, towards some kind of perfection. And here is the chance this land, in this country. Whether we will grab it, I don't know.

BILL: Joan, you said that America looks at you as Black first and American second. Isn't that the way you think of yourself?

ALEX: Sure.

AILEEN: Yes!

JOAN: Definitely.

ALEX: But there's a danger in that. You know how it was in the '70's when there had been big battles to get Black youngsters into universities, and when they got there, they got the "Black House" and the Black Studies and all that. There were reasons, of course. Yet the end result was that they ostracized themselves. They became paranoid Black. However justified it was, their only concern was blackness. Everything else was irrelevant chemistry, physics, and so forth. I see it in Hollywood too. Writers who might be very good writers if they would just go ahead and let themselves be writers. But they are almost incapable of thinking without thinking Black. It appalls me.

JOAN: Alex, I want to tell you what your book did for my family. My family left the South in 1916, and in leaving the pain of their experience there behind them, they eliminated it completely from their lives. Even from their vocabulary. I never ate greens or cornbread, for instance. Even when they fixed them, they didn't name them. And I told the teacher I was English because I thought whatever language you spoke, that's what you were. My family never discussed what we were or where we came from.

ALEX: *Yes, that happens.*

JOAN: *Then your book came out, and I bought a copy for everyone in the family, and they started talking. That's when I realized what a rich heritage they had kept from me because of their great pain. I could understand why they did it, and it gave me an extra dimension of love and respect and admiration for them, and for the fact that they had survived. And I remembered an old African proverb I had read never despise a bridge over which you have walked.*

GINETTA: *What a lovely proverb!*

JOAN: *So, Alex, I want to thank you on behalf of, I'm sure, millions and millions of Black families to whom your book has meant so much.*

ALEX: *You know, a big concern of Doubleday's was that Black people wouldn't buy the book because Black people aren't known as hardcover book buyers. Well, the first book signing was at a shopping center in Los Angeles, and I was told there might be five hundred people there. Instead, there were close to five thousand. So all I could do was sit there and sign my name. I hadn't time to look up and see these people. I just saw a pair of hands put a book in front of me. And I began to look at the hands, the range of hands: Finely manicured, knobby knuckles, cracked with grease under the nails, Black hands, Oriental hands, white hands. And it was uncanny how I could look at a pair of hands so many like that and I knew that pair of hands had never bought a book before.*

JOAN: *Oh, that's exciting! What a wonderful story.*

ALEX: *Then at a signing in New York, there was a Black lady, probably about seventy, dressed not shabbily but just this side of it. With one glance at her, I knew her lineage, and I knew she had no business buying seven books. Then I saw her go into her bank—the bank of an old Black woman, her bosom.*

PAT: *My mother did that too.*

ALEX: *I saw that lady count out whatever it was, eighty dollars, to buy those seven books. And I sort of got up out of the chair. I didn't want her to pay. But she said, "Now, son, don't you worry. I ain't buying books. I'm buying our history." Well, I tell you the truth. I sat down and I was crying. I was signing books with tears running down my face.*

JOAN: *I can understand that. I am near tears just hearing about it.*

PAT: *We all are.*

ALEX: *Another moving thing, I found it among Blacks, whites, and Orientals. Older people would come up with several books and ask you to autograph them to their children. And younger people would buy books and ask you to autograph them to their parents and grandparents. It had nothing to do with race. The generations in families of all races were communicating through the book.*

AILEEN: *That doesn't happen a lot these days, that kind of communication.*

ALEX: *No, it doesn't. With the automobile and television, we've moved away from the time that wasn't all that long ago when the entertainment of families all over the world used to consist largely of family gatherings in the evenings. And the elders talked and the young ones listened. That's gone now, more or less. But every time we pull further away from our roots, from our elders, it sets up a strain in us. We miss the stability. And I think that's sort of what the book touched. For everybody, not just Blacks. And this*

*happened without my knowing it. I sure didn't know that was what
I was doing.*

MARCIA: *But that's what you did, all right. You spoke to the desire
in all of us to have roots and a family. We've come too far from
the family, I think, and now people are trying to get back.*

There comes time at most Roundtables, usually over coffee, when
silence replaces conversation. It's not an awkward, embarrassed
silence, imposed because no one has any more to say. It's pregnant
with unexpressed words, thoughts, and emotions. It's as if people
have to absorb what's been said as they digest their food. They
need time and space to incorporate new thoughts and new feelings and new relationships into themselves. As hostess, I respect
that need. It's my need too.

But this day, with the rain pounding at the windows, I was impressed with the warmth of the silence around the table. It was as
if we were a family that had found itself.

CHAPTER FOURTEEN

1978

Sex and Society

The table on this sunny day in San Francisco had been expanded to accommodate a wheelchair. One of my guests, Gaye Blackford, a former nurse, was coping with M.S. (Multiple Sclerosis), which felled her rather quickly. Now she was writing a book about her experience with the intractable disease. I admired her bravery in continuing to grow to write and encourage others. The week before the luncheon, knowing Gaye would attend the Roundtable, I listened to therapists talk about the issues of having an active sex life while living with catastrophic disease.

PAT: *A friend took me to hear therapists who were meeting for a three-day seminar and convention as he thought it might be something I could write about for my column. So I went over, and we walked into a dark room where they were showing a film that happened to be about sex and the disabled. I was curious in view of the fact that Gaye was coming to lunch today and she is writing a book on this very subject.*

GAYE: *And I've seen these and I don't like those films. I've seen The Fuck-Around in film festivals. I've seen fifty million of them.*

PAT: *Now I don't know about that. I wouldn't put that title on it at all. It was the most pornographic film I've ever seen. They left absolutely nothing to one's imagination. And I was sitting there sort of with my mouth open, watching this film in the dark,* *obviously not one of them. They were just ordinary-looking people. I don't know why I thought sex therapists would look any different, but I did. But they spotted me right away. And they came over to me and said, "Where's your name tag?" I said, "I don't have one I'm with the press." So I had to leave, but not before I had seen the film. And you, Gaye, are writing this book. Would you tell us how you got involved with this and why you're writing it?*

GAYE: *Alright and I'll say a couple of things about me. I am a nurse. I am a graduate of UC Medical Center. Two weeks before my junior year of nursing school, in May of '63 I started having difficulty walking and I didn't know what was happening. They diagnosed me with multiple sclerosis. I was in a wheel chair by Christmas of '63. It was very fast. When I completed my bachelor's degree I immediately went on to get my master's*

GUESTS

Dr. Carl Djerassi • Father of the birth control pill; author and playwright

George Davis • Attorney at Law

Mimi Silbert • Psychologist and co-president of Delancey Street, a successful organization for the rehabilitation of ex-convicts. Mimi also works with the police department.

Aileen Hernandez • Women's rights activist; urban consultant; past national president of N.O.W.

Joan Luther • Longtime restaurant publicist

Ken Washington

Gaye Blackford • Former nurse

Aundrea • Advisor to a Los Angeles rape treatment center

degree. And I've taught courses through continuing education and nursing. I was temporarily hired to gather published literature on sexuality, spinal cord injuries and multiple sclerosis. I read all of the literature on these diseases and I added many, many more conditions. And I've seen The Fuck-Around at these festivals, which I'm sure, is what you're talking about.

AILEEN: *Say that again?*

MIMI: *That's really an unnecessary title to give this.*

AILEEN: *Is that the title?*

GAYE: *Yes.*

PAT: *When I was growing up, if that word had been used, I would have fainted and fallen on the floor and been dead.*

GAYE: *But it's very disease-specific. They didn't have specific disease information. Every chapter is a different medical description. The heart chapter is divided into six different chapters of heart conditions.*

DR. CARL: *Do you have a good index in your book?*

GAYE: *Yes.*

PAT: *Where do you get all of your information?*

GAYE: *I'm running an awful lot of med lines through the National Library of Medicine. And I'm just doing a lot of interviewing.*

PAT: *I think that most people never think of someone who is disabled as being a sexual person. And that's a myth, obviously. And especially after seeing that film I realize that it was certainly a myth. It was more sexual than anything I had ever encountered in my life.*

GAYE: *But I think it is a very interesting, very thorough book. And certainly well needed, I mean there's no question. In the last 20 years our culture has gone through some major changes, and* *more importantly, our openness and expression of feelings. I came here a year ago and I've known for some time that everything is coming out of the closet. But I think that on a national level, on the subject of sexuality, Americans, we as a culture, have come a long way. But we have a long way to go. And it's interesting that here in San Francisco, the fact that we have an association of sexual therapists in the country, in large numbers, says something about the strides that we haven't made in sexuality.*

PAT: *Does the subject of sexuality make any of your uncomfortable?*

AILEEN: *It bores me to tears.*

PAT: *Does it?*

AILEEN: *I'm getting so sick and tired of having everybody involved in every single issue of sexuality. This, [particular subject on disability] doesn't bore me because I think that's going to be a significant addition to the information. But I think every conversation has to do with sexuality. It's as if that's the only thing we're involved in in our lives.*

DR. CARL: *Every once in a while I teach a course at Stanford that has to deal with the bio-social aspects of birth control. These are upperclassmen. We are dividing them into groups and studying them. One of the main problems, particularly with teenagers and young people that we deal with is that parents do not talk about sex with their children. There was not one student in that group who said they were comfortable talking with their parents about sex. We're not talking here about birth control alone; we're talking particularly about sexuality. And I think that's indispensable.*

AILEEN: *I think that's very important. And I believe that if you took any group in this society you would find the exact same information. Very few people have communicated with their parents—*

KEN: *It's not much of a lack of information as it is people being uncomfortable about it. People are pretending it doesn't occur.*

AILEEN: *Well that is not what I'm talking about when I say I'm bored with the subject. You almost never hear anybody talk about anything else anymore. Maybe it's San Francisco that makes that true. But you don't go anywhere without having people discuss sexuality as if it's the only dimension of a human being. Everybody seems to only talk about this now as if this is the only area of a human being. Your sexuality is part of you. It is not the only thing about you.*

GAYE: *When you're talking major diseases, it's very complicated. The couple becomes very aware of what's going on. When the couple knows the woman is brittle, they're seriously abstinent.*

AILEEN: *I think we are in the process now of learning a lot more than we have ever learned before simply because there has been a willingness to communicate, even if it's incorrect communications. And a lot of it, I think, has been incorrect communication. I guess maybe it's just the places I'm going lately. I look at all the rest of the world and all the issues that are left there to deal with. And we spend so much time in this community.*

PAT: *It is one of the more pleasant ones.*

AILEEN: *Maybe that's the reason we talk about it, because it's more pleasant than others.*

KEN: *To my mind it's a question of friendship. If you can begin with this element of intense friendship with another person and you're not afraid of that, then the sexual aspects of it become very natural and comfortable. It's been my observation that most people are afraid of intense friendships anyway.*

PAT: *Well we're all afraid to reveal ourselves aren't we? Isn't that a basic human feeling? We feel we have to have a façade?*

Ken: Well you reach a point where you say: "What the hell does it matter? Whom do I owe it to?" I mean I don't let it all hang out. What's the point in that? That's boring. I don't have anything to hide. Then the rest just seems to come.

MIMI: *It's funny because these days there really are people who can talk apparently openly about such things as sexuality as a way of avoiding anything personal or intense. And to me that is quite boring.*

MIMI: *The whole idea of what you're doing is wonderful. Because those are the kinds of facts that people don't know and they feel so silly asking.*

AILEEN: *The same thing is true about age. Age and sex has been something that has been under the table for a long time too. The assumption is that when you hit age "whatever" that sexuality just disappears.*

PAT: *And that's true for both men and women.*

AILEEN: *Yes, very much so.*

MIMI: *And I find that very different from the discussion of whether whipped cream on my nose is particularly appealing.*

AILEEN: *Maybe that's what I'm bored with: the topic of everybody's sexual athletics as opposed to sexuality as a topic.*

MIMI: *Well how do you count for the proliferation of manuals and books with techniques? You can count the number of books in the last 10 or 15 years that have become bestsellers.*

AILEEN: *Well because I think there's a great thirst for understanding those things. It sells.*

PAT: *Because in the past, sex has not been considered a nice thing to do unless you're married. And you're not supposed to have sex until you are married.*

AILEEN: *But the writing of these books on this subject has proved to be lucrative.*

PAT: Well I've never been involved in a conversation that has dealt with sexuality. You say you're bored by it and I have never been involved in that kind of conversation except in an intimate way, with one other person.

AILEEN: This was THE topic of conversation in the women's movement for years. You could not go to a meeting without, inevitably, discussing sexuality.

PAT: Wasn't that because of the lesbian issue?

AILEEN: It wasn't just the lesbian issue. It goes back to your contribution Dr. Djerassi, if you will, and that is the control that women then had over the processes of birth by looking at the pill and other things that could be used; and the release from feeling negative about their sexuality. A great part about the women's movement was the sexual freedom of women. Not lesbianism as such. That was one portion of it. But the fact that women could then control themselves and their bodies and everything else, they were free to feel sexual.

PAT: But you've been in a unique position in terms of being the second national president of the National Organization for Women. And also being terribly involved in the movement. I've been involved in feminism. But I haven't been involved in the movement.

AILEEN: I think there is less discussion in the Black community on sexuality than in almost any other community.

PAT: Why is that?

AILEEN: I think many Black people have resented for many years the stereotypical approach to Blacks that they were only sensual human beings. So in terms of discussing, it's something you don't talk about. We were doing some seminars the other day with an agency of state government. And we've done stereotypes with a lot of groups. And they talked about the super-stud, etc. So then

they asked: "Are there any stereotypes about white males?" So the
few women and minorities in the group, who could talk, looked
at stereotypes [for white males]. And one of the ones that came
up was immoral. And they were flabbergasted that anyone would
consider white males immoral, because it's not the concept.

MIMI: That was part of the profile of white males?

AILEEN: Yes, part of the profile of white males is that they are
extremely immoral. And it's across a bunch of lines. It isn't just in
terms of sex; it's across a bunch of other issues as well. And I just
believe that maybe we need to talk more in the Black community
about sexuality and take it from our point of view instead of
having it laid upon us by other people in our society. It's been such
a negative concept.

MIMI: But do you think those myths have been exploded?

AILEEN: No, I don't think they've been exploded. I think there
are lots of whites that still think that Blacks are primarily
sensual, animalistic human beings who copulate anywhere and
everywhere, at the drop of a hat. I think there are lots of people
who believe that our stereotypes almost never come up with
anything intellectual on Blacks. Almost everything on Blacks is
physical.

DR. CARL: But what about some of the novelists: Alice Walker, Toni
Morrison, James Baldwin and others. They indeed have created
figures and characters, which add a little bit of fuel to support that
stereotype. Bigger Thomas, for instance, in "Native Son"—

AILEEN: Yes. Which is a very old book.

CARL: Well it is. But it is a classic in the canon of 20th century
American literature. And the characters that live in the novel—

KEN: He was sort of a pathetic character. Not a self-motivated
character; more of a victim than anything.

AILEEN: *[Blacks] don't have real life in every novel that's been put out, or enough of a slice of life, to show differences. And I think people will buy books that are heavily sexually laden. You know, the Mandingo novels.*

KEN: *If that particular image were to be reinforced, I think it's reinforced more in the newspapers. I've noticed a resurgence of what we used to call "race-baiting" in The Examiner. For example, last week just after the assassination attempt, The Examiner gave an example of public comment on the street. And the person who had given the positive comment said it was a terrible thing, and they were a white person. And the person who said that it was justified was a Black person.*

PAT: *I'm very sorry to hear that, that's my paper.*

KEN: *Yeah it's a great paper from some standpoints. I read The Examiner every day.*

AILEEN: *San Francisco does not have a great paper.*

PAT: *No, it doesn't. It's better than The Chronicle. Put it that way.*

KEN: *Yes it has a wider view than The Chronicle. But I find a lot of these types of stereotypical presentations in The Examiner. And I find it a bit distressing. Because, on the same day, another paper had six people giving their views on the assassination. And it was a pretty balanced group. But I never find this in The Examiner. I just really never do. And it's distressing. And I think that's a bit more heinous than seeing it in a novel.*

GAYE: *Because of the heart chapter, I'm covering stroke. And I'm a member of the Stroke Club with the American Heart Association. Bernard Shaw, out of the San Francisco Police Department, was giving a speech on violence prevention to the Stroke Club. I didn't realize that there were a growing number of male rapes that were not homosexual.*

PAT: *What do you mean it isn't homosexual?*

MIMI: *Meaning it's not necessarily being performed by a gay man. Any man, gay or straight, can be attacked by anyone walking down the street.*

PAT: *Aundrea deals with rape in terms of the rape treatment center in Los Angeles.*

AUNDREA: *Well I have kind of an interesting perspective on that. In my other life I'm married to the district attorney of Los Angeles County. And one day, about two years ago, a very delightful young woman comes to my office saying: "I went to see your husband and he tells me I should come see you." Her name is Gail Gardnell. She is a social worker. She is interested in rape ramifications for women and treatment of families of the victim and people around the victim as well. She works at Santa Monica hospital. And over the years they have taken on countless rape patients. Then it extended into a rape treatment center for victims. She came to me saying she needed $70,000 a year for her to keep this center going. She was training other women and other social workers in hospitals around the Los Angeles area. I helped her put together an advising team. Each year we put on a major fundraiser that I think helped a lot of families deal with rape over the years.*

PAT: *Have you ever dealt with male rape victim?*

AUNDREA: *Personally, no. The treatment center has. It's very traumatic.*

MIMI: *It really is tremendously on the rise.*

AILEEN: *If you look at rape as being a crime of hostility rather than sex, it could follow very easily that it could be that way.*

AUNDREA: *That's the point of this whole center. I didn't realize that, that it's not a sexual crime. And we've had rape victims come and talk about it. And they all emphasize the same point: that it is not a sexual crime. And to hear men at this point come in and* *listen and respond to the situation, it's had a great deal of impact. And with that you're going to have some action on a long-term basis.*

MIMI: *I just finished a study on 200 prostitutes in the Bay Area. The findings on rape were one of the most astounding. I separated rape having anything to do with their job, which is to say a customer forcing issues beyond what they contracted for. And we focused on rape simply happening to them as people. Over 73% of them (most of them were juveniles) were raped primarily because they were on the streets at bad times of night. The vast majority were "stranger rapes" unlike the general population. One of the really fascinating points was there were a significant number of them who told the rapist—in the course of the rape— to calm down, there's no reason for this. Let me just turn you a free trick. Instead of calming the rapist, in every single case, it inflamed them. Their physical injuries were significantly greater. There was not one of those cases that didn't end up with severe injuries and broken bones. The rapist just went totally out of control and found it necessary to increase the crime from simply rape to attempted murder, and in some cases: pistol whippings. It's one of the first things I've read that has a clear cut separation on the rape and violence issue in which the sex was overtly offered to calm what they thought was violence.*

GAYE: *Also Bernard Shaw was saying that there are an enormous number of divorces after rapes and he highly recommended getting into counseling after rape.*

PAT: *And why is that? Why would there be a high rate of divorce after rape?*

AUNDREA: *There's a feeling that the woman has somehow invited this.*

PAT: *That's the old way of looking at this.*

AUNDREA: *Well anyone at this table is a potential victim.*

PAT: *I would dare to say that almost everyone at this table has been raped. I had a Roundtable where we did talk about it individually. But there are different kinds of rape. It all depends on the definition of rape. Because rape, more often than not, happens with people we know.*

AILEEN: *Even in a marriage, the assumption is that a wife is available for her husband whenever he chooses.*

PAT: *George, you're on. As a very famous lawyer who has handled all kinds of cases...*

GEORGE: *Very frankly this is all kind of funny to me. I'm sitting here wondering whether you're all being naïve or whether you're just not there. You talk about male rapes, go down to the county jail; the same thing is going on. I have clients who dread the thought of going to prison, not because they dread being confined, they dread the thought of being raped the day they get there. I don't understand why you guys don't realize you're victims of your own educational background and your cultural background. And again this is an opinion; I don't mean to be vicious about it. It just seems to me that we're all victims. I grew up under the Christian ethic. And I think most of our education is so stupid. Why don't they talk in school about things like this? I've gone to other countries in this world and I've lived there. People talk about sex, they train their children how to be wives, how to be good to their partners. It's part of the educational system. You're just in the wrong country that's all.*

DR. CARL: *I'm interested in what countries you're talking about.*

GEORGE: *Well Japan is one. I just came back from a place where they said: "You've had your dinner and your drink, now how about a woman?" They say, "Well you've eaten; don't you want to have sex?"*

AILEEN: *Well does it work the other way around? If I were to go over there would they say that to me?*

DR. CARL: *You're talking about a very specific segment of the male Japanese establishment.*

GEORGE: *The old Chinese, Thailand, Viet Nam . . . all of those countries have a different attitude about sex than we do. And they think sex is really normal and natural; something that you need.*

DR. CARL: *But you're talking about incredible minorities here. If you look at Japan; Japan does not consist of just businessmen that travel around.*

GEORGE: *Well I don't say you're all wrong. But I think it goes back to our schools, frankly. How are you ever going to change the situation if you don't have educational programs that are geared up to what's important in life. I think most of our education is so stupid. Not all of it. But why don't they talk about this type of thing in our schools?*

MIMI: *I think that goes back to the home though.*

AILEEN: *At home they don't talk about these things.*

CHAPTER FIFTEEN

1978

Sex and Society
(continued)

GEORGE: A would-be client accused of rape asked me to represent him I said what was this all about? He said he was giving her therapy. He's a doctor, he said he felt that she was lonesome; and needed some feeling of love and affection.

GAYE: Was this a patient?

GEORGE: Yes. She was there for a patient interview and then he felt that this was a form of treatment.

GAYE: There was a speech by a reporter a couple of years ago about the growing number of rapes by psychiatrists to their patients.

GEORGE: Well you call it rape but the jury called it consensual sexual intercourse. Now I'll tell you something interesting here in San Francisco. Do you know that a rape case is the worst case to defend? And it's a much more difficult case to defend in San Francisco, right now, than a murder case.

PAT: Why?

GEORGE: Because people are so hung up on it. They're walking around acting as though rape is some kind of an offense, that really every rapist ought to be executed. It's a psychological thing. And I think it's a part of the malaise of people generally. We're sick. This is a sick society. Maybe everyone around this table is *healthy and not sick. But most of the people that you deal with in this society are sick. They're frustrated. They're angry. They're violent. They're vicious. The crimes that are committed now, they're not like the crimes that were committed when I first started to practice law, which was 50 years ago.*

KEN: *There's such a thing as a pure crime. And crimes today definitely are not the same.*

(Laughter)

GEORGE: *I know it's generalizing, but what I mean to say is that people are killing people because they're mad at them. They're shooting them because they're angrier. The other day I read about a car that stopped and the fella hadn't turned his blinker on. The fella in the back got out of his car and started to castigate [the man in front] because he was mad that he hadn't turned his blinker on. And the fella in the front car got out, reached in the back, and pulled a gun out, shot and killed him and drove off. And what kind of crime is that? That's a sick society that commits those kinds of crimes.*

KEN: *I would agree that there are indeed, maybe more so than any other time in our country's development, more frustrated individuals. And they are good people in the best sense. But their level of frustration has reach—*

GEORGE: *Well you see nothing but corruption around you in all forms of life, and public life especially. People are holding jobs and they're doing nothing. They're spending money. The whole society is sick. And people are frustrated because there's nothing they can do. What can you do about it? You read in the paper, some fella gets a lifetime pension because he says he has a heart failure. Look at all of these goofy cases.*

AILEEN: *And it adds to the stress of the dollar.*

GEORGE: *Yes. And if you're going to give everybody everything* *they ask for, we're going to be a bankrupt society. Nobody seems to think they can do anything about it. Nobody cares. So we sit around here and talk about sex . . . but that should've been over half an hour ago.*

MIMI: *I think it's one thing to make a statement about a bankrupt society, and a bankrupt country. But the bankruptcy of the spirit is something that is much more devastating.*

GEORGE: *That's at the bottom of it, that's really at the bottom of it.*

KEN: *I don't agree. I think that what we've been talking about is the strain that's run through everything. We started out talking about people who couldn't talk to each other about a very basic subject. It's really the question of alienation that does indeed run through our society, and it always has. I don't see any clear evidence that it's any different today in degree than it was a hundred years ago. I mean a hundred years ago we had a civil war. We had one part of the country totally against the other. I don't see that there's a significant difference. We have leaders in this country that don't understand sometimes what the country is all about; and are willing to sell us short. I think there was a real opportunity for cohesion seven years ago when Nixon was pardoned. I think at that point, everybody was focused on a major wrong in the society. And everyone was focused at the same time, and then it was pulled out from under us. And I see a certain frustration that occurred time and time again since that. Maybe that's just one point amongst several. Then we have the situation you were talking about. I know you see that a lot. I read about those situations it seems like every three months. We have newspaper reporters that are sharper and things are getting reported more.*

PAT: *A lot of things have come out of the closet too that we were hiding before. Rape for instance.*

MIMI: *Also, it's the change of classes. And that's perhaps the difference. The poor have always felt frustrated. The poor have* *always been helpless. The poor have always been out of control of their lives. And the poor have been the ones who have been involved in these crimes. And right now the middle class feels frustrated. The middle class is out of control and suddenly the middle class is shooting people and everyone is saying oh my god things are changing. NO but the class of people is changing. They're killing people.*

KEN: *I don't necessarily agree.*

MIMI: *Oh I think the middle class is involved in more white-collar crime. The class of people is changing. See the middle class was always involved in the crime. The middle class has access to more white-collar crime and manipulates crimes. And now I think they are involved in the spontaneous, nothing-to-lose kind of crimes. These have really, for years, have been the problems of the poor.*

PAT: *But to go back to something you were saying George because I think you're dismissing this rape thing very lightly. And I would wonder, that if you were a woman, and you had been raped, how would you feel? I think it would be a very different matter.*

GEORGE: *Oh you bet. I would feel traumatized.*

PAT: *And in the past, women have not reported rape because they have ended up not only the victim, but also the one who has been accused of enticing the person who raped them. So it was hidden. We now have come out of the closet about this and we are saying: "We were raped!" "I was raped."—whomever it may be.*

GEORGE: *Well I agree with you. I couldn't agree with you more on that.*

PAT: *So that's not something that has changed, in terms of the amount of rape. It's something that's changed in terms of us saying something about it now. Because finally something can be done.*

GAYE: *According to Bernard Shaw, if you think women don't report rape male rapes are something they never mention.*

KEN: *I can't imagine how I would report if a man raped me. Regarding what you just said about a man being raped by another man, a year ago I would have laughed at that. But I had a strange experience over the past year. I was in a situation where an old friend essentially accosted me. And because I refused to call the police just to get her out, I was in sort of a no-win situation. And I understood rape for the first time. And I could see if it were a physical question of being overpowered, the feeling would have been much the same.*

PAT: *Yes. We're suddenly facing these things and talking about them and learning from them.*

AILEEN: *We're learning a lot more from a number of situations. I think that's great. I'm still bored with this point that we're talking about. Because I think it's very easy for people to talk about this and much less easy to talk about a lot of other things that we've got to communicate about, which we're not talking about.*

PAT: *What would you like to talk about Aileen?*

AILEEN: *Almost everything else in this society.*

(Laughter)

PAT: *What's important to you at this point?*

AILEEN: *I'm listening to some of the things Mimi said for example. And I'm very concerned about where the country is going in terms of its approach to those who cannot survive in this society. This is a nation that has said "survival of the fittest" therefore if you don't survive, it's clear you're not fit. I'm concerned about that. I'm concerned about an attitude that says the government should remove itself from everything that involves dealing with those who are least capable of helping themselves in this society. And that's what we're saying now.*

PAT: *That is what's being said now. That's true.*

AILEEN: *And yet these very same people who are saying it can go back, if they were honest, and look at an awful lot of things that the government has helped them with over the past. But they've forgotten it all. Nobody wants to remember the GI Bill of Rights, which was the biggest welfare system that we've ever had. It was a huge welfare program for veterans.*

DR. CARL: *Do you feel the same way on a global context? Or, focusing on America, the fact that we are doing less and less in context of foreign aid then—*

AILEEN: *I feel very strongly about that. I think we're doing less and less in terms of helping foreign aid and more and more in terms of military foreign aid. Which I think is a total disaster for the country. I'm tired of watching the male leaders of this society flex their muscles over who's the most macho.*

DR. CARL: *What do you try to do about this as a woman?*

PAT: *As a very powerful woman, actually.*

AILEEN: *I do all that I can do about this. I speak out on it. I belong to a number of organizations that focus on this area. I scream whenever I get a chance to scream. But I find myself, very often, sounding like the only voice in this. I hear people telling me that American has to survive therefore we must do this. We have to challenge Russia to a hill top confrontation, because if they don't, then the communists are going to be right here at our doorstep tomorrow. El Salvador is our issue because if we don't stop them in El Salvador, we'll have to stop them at the San Francisco Golden Gate.*

MIMI: *And if we don't start a war in El Salvador, we won't be able to change our economy the way we promised to.*

JOAN: *Don't you think there's a difference between challenging and being protected with your strength?*

AILEEN: *I do not believe that the United States is without strength.*

I just don't believe that. I believe we have enough strength to
do anything that we choose to do. I think where our strength
is lacking is in the personal strength and the national strength
in terms of our commitment. I just don't believe that the US is
in danger from communism. I think that we're in danger from
something worse than communism. And that is: our own lack of
understanding about who we are as a people.

MIMI: And also a lack of purpose and values.

JOAN: Everyone's lost their values.

MIMI: Boy, whoever started the phrase about "I don't want to
impose my values on you," I'd like to find that person and impose
a few of my own values on them. I think that was one of the most
dangerous spreads run across our country. And it left us incredibly
weak with a fiber full of holes. And there's no question that we're
playing on that fear in every way possible, with our responses
to crime and internal things. Like, you were saying, you can't
defend anybody these days. Everybody suddenly is hot Law and
Order. And that's the fear of all of those holes. And it's true with
our foreign policy as well. We're immediately flexing because we
sense our own weakness. And instead of making ourselves strong,
we run quickly to what we remember as our strengths from way
back when. I think we're in the middle of a nervous breakdown.

GEORGE: Well I'm getting to be very pessimistic about our judicial
system. I've been working at it all my life and I've been using it
and I've been manipulating it. Because when I started it was at
the other end of the spectrum and everybody was getting their
head beaten in with pipes and what not. And nobody had any
protection. And so the lawyers of my early days had a real zeal.
We had a real purpose in life. We were protecting people. But I
must admit it's gone so far the other way now, that I read these
cases that come out of the Supreme Court and I'm embarrassed.
I'm embarrassed when I read about a fella who confessed to

committing a crime. And he did it five minutes later as the statute said it would be admissible. And so for that purpose, he's free. I tell ya', I'm looking at this thing and I'm saying to myself: maybe the system is outmoded. Maybe this system that was created 200 years ago, in an entirely different kind of society that our society today is—

JOAN: *A different kind of American character?*

GEORGE: *The whole picture of society is a different society. It isn't working. They're saying: use more judges. You can't use more judges. They won't get any work done. Longer jail terms don't mean a thing. They don't deter anything. You got to get down to the bottom; that basic element of life: the family. If you don't get back to the family; if you don't get back to the schools; if you don't' get back to the authority; if you don't' get back to training. . . . We're going down the road that every other society has gone down all through history when this has happened to them.*

PAT: *I do have to agree with you. I feel that the family is terribly important. And I feel that our families are disrupted. All families seem to be disrupted by divorce, by not caring, by no commitment.*

KEN: *On the way here I was having a discussion with a cab driver. I was saying I love San Francisco; he was talking about how he grew up here. And he was saying he was moving. He's moving because he grew up in a San Francisco that had strong neighborhoods. He was observing—and I was observing as well—that there is a phenomenon that has happened in this town—and I'm sure it's happened in many across the country—where you've had the destruction of neighborhoods for economic reasons. Now I'm an investor and I'm involved in things like that. So I love development and new projects. But until we develop an ethic in our country— starting on a local level—that says there's a priority with families, we have an obligation to try to preserve neighborhoods where* families can flourish. These things aren't going to change. We can't say: ok trans-America you can wipe out twenty families on block X-Y-Z, you know? [We can't just] wholesale without any concern. We'll have these discussions for the next 90 years and lament the breakdown in families and all of the rest of the things that come about when family structure deteriorates. So how do we balance off those issues? And that's what's happening in this town. I believe it's eastern developers that have come into this town and started to break up neighborhoods and it's impossible—

PAT: Not just eastern developers. First of all we're a city. And we do have to consider that we ARE a city. We do have to have areas for families and homes and that kind of thing. But at the same time we have to remember that we need growth as a city. That's important too, isn't it?

KEN: So how do you balance off the two? That's all I'm saying. It's an issue. It's a problem.

PAT: It *is* a problem.

KEN: All of us want to see growth. That's the American ethic.

PAT: George is having a fit over there.

GEORGE: As I told you before I came, I have to be down at court at 2:00.

DR. DJERASSI: The man is guilty.

(Laughter)

PAT: George, probably the best case I know you for is my own. But besides that, before you go, can you tell us about the Carl Chessman case? Do you consider that, still, as one of your most famous cases?

GEORGE: Sure. I'll tell you a secret thought I have now. I'm going to try to call The Examiner one of these days—because they're going to start executing again, I think, pretty soon.

MIMI: Yes.

GEORGE: And now the reporters have got the freedom of the press, and they can go in the courtrooms. Now I've always been against capital punishment, but I think I'm going to have to take a different tactic. I'd like to be hired for a dollar to represent the examiner.

PAT: Here's a dollar.

GEORGE: And I'd like to insist that we be allowed to go in the prison, interview the prisoners the night before, check out their last meals and see what they're eating, go in and photograph the executions. And let everybody see what capital punishment is. That's what everybody's voting for. And I think we should be able to go interview the prisoners and let everyone know all about it. See I was there the night before Chessman died. He wrote a couple of letters. You can't get into executions. You have to be subpoenaed. It's a limited number of people. If it's a police killer, more policemen are allowed in. But I'd like to see if it opened up to the public.

PAT: But that was very popular. Remember when they had public hangings? And everyone brought their children and they had picnics. But it was not a deterrent. Well George, I always ask a personal question. I'm kind of moving along into this, because I just moved into the country this weekend. And I find it a very traumatic thing. And I think about all of the moves we make in our lives and what they mean to us. And if indeed you've made moves in your life that have been traumatic . . . how? How has this affected you?

GEORGE: Well I'll give you my answer briefly. I'm an optimist. And I believe in mind over matter and I don't bother about those kinds of things. I could walk out of here tomorrow and hear about a lot of tragedy and just wipe it right out of my mind and go right on. Because I don't think any of us are immune from it. And I think the *only thing that will remain, no matter what we do, is time. There's nothing else. I think the only thing that will remain after anything we do is time.*

PAT: *But you have your own personal feelings. You can't ignore how you're feeling. Or can you?*

GEORGE: *No. Well I had a terrible feeling about a year ago. I had a horse. I thought it was the best horse I had ever owned in my life. And it died, through the fault of the people who were keeping it. My wife died a few years back. I've had a normal run of tragedies and I don't think there's any answer to it except to just wipe it out and keep on going. If you're just going to sit around moping about what happened . . . well goodbye. I don't want to see you; I don't want to talk to you. I don't have time for it. I'm really glad to meet all of you, but I must go.*

PAT: *Mr. Davis, before you leave I must ask you this one last question. You said earlier that you were just teasing all of us. Were you really just teasing?*

GEORGE: *Oh sort of.*

DR. DJERASSI: *What percentage of it was teasing?*

(Laughter)

GEORGE: *To the extent that you want to think I was teasing you, you can think that. And to the extent that you think I wasn't, you can think that too.*

PAT: *I think you were dead serious.*

AILEEN: *What a great lawyer you are.*

GEORGE: *Listen I'm glad to meet all of you. I'd like to know you better. You can't come to something like this without wanting to know everybody. I'm sorry I just have to get out of here. Bye. Thanks for letting me come here.*

After George left, we felt the gap that his departure left in our conversation.

KEN: *We've lost our protagonist.*

AILEEN: *[There's] too much unanimity around the rest of the table. You haven't said a word Joan. You'll have to include yourself in this discussion.*

JOAN: *I'm not very qualified in these discussions. I'm disqualified.*

PAT: *Yes Joan you've been extremely quiet. We're going to put you on the spot.*

JOAN: *I'll tell you I'm not a great theorist. I live by the day and I'm going to be terribly honest about something: I think there's far too many emphasis placed on sex. I'll put it this way: I'm a big career girl. I walked down the aisle at 18 years old with the only man I ever loved. That was 33 years ago. The status quo is still the same. I've never been raped or any attempt. And I don't know what you all are talking about.*

PAT: *Then you've led a very sheltered life.*

JOAN: *I am totally ignorant and I'm sorry to be that way.*

MIMI: *Are you sorry to be that way or glad to be that way?*

JOAN: *May not because I could care less. That's my honest to god opinion. I'm not interested.*

KEN: *There's no sin in that either.*

MIMI: *I would give anything not to know some of the things I know.*

JOAN: *I've been talking to one of my dear friends. I can tell her anything I like. But I don't want to talk about sex. I think it's boring. [There are] too many other things to talk about.*

KEN: *You'd better not say that, that's what initiated the other conversation.*

(Laughter)

AILEEN: *I think I was guilty with that one.*

JOAN: *I really mean this. I grew up never caring, I was the only child. I adored my father. I grew up on the volleyball and basketball field. And then I got married. And my head is not there and never has been there.*

PAT: *What is important to you, Joan?*

KEN: *I'd like to know what your perspective is? That's a radically different perspective than most of the world knows.*

JOAN: *I'm sorry. I'm not a feminist. I've been in business for 30 years and I've never felt a sting. And some of best friends, I can't even feel them. I'm almost embarrassed.*

DR. DJERASSI: *Do you have any children?*

JOAN: *No I never have, Doctor. That may be another reason.*

DR. DJERASSI: *Well let me ask you this question, since you don't have children. Why do you think the institution of marriage is important in the absence of children?*

JOAN: *Anybody can tell me anything; I've been sitting her thinking what a lousy Catholic I've come up to be. Nuns reared me. In retrospect, I never agreed about birth control.*

PAT: *In the Catholic church?*

JOAN: *Yes. I couldn't do it. I still couldn't do it. Well, I'm so old now; I don't have to worry about it anymore.*

PAT: *Couldn't do what? Couldn't use birth control?*

JOAN: *I wonder Pat. It's never been a problem. I cannot say because I grew up as a Catholic. I don't know, I never been put to* the test. I've never had to worry about it. I will say this to you: I'm positive I could not ever have an abortion.

PAT: Joan, you haven't answered the question. Would you answer the question?

JOAN: Excuse me for wandering. What I think I was getting at is: I like my husband and he's my best friend.

DR. DJERASSI: But I don't question that at all. I'm just saying: why can't you live with him without being married?

JOAN: Can't do it.

DR. DJERASSI: I've gathered that you can't, but I'm wondering: why? That's what I meant.

JOAN: I don't know why. The only thing I can answer you is: being very honest, I could never sleep with another man while being married to Bill Luther. Now if Bill Luther died, maybe that commitment could disappear.

DR. DJERASSI: I'm not talking about monogamy versus anything else. I'm talking about you maintaining a strictly monogamous relationship with one man—

JOAN: Well I'm committed to marriage, Doctor.

DR. DJERASSI: Can you explain to me what is important about marriage?

JOAN: I'm living with a man that I adore and he's my best friend. I love him.

DR. DJERASSI: But couldn't you adore him and not be married to him.

JOAN: Well yes! Of course. I'm married to him.

MIMI: Well I'm going to take her side on this. Why should she live with him not married?

PAT: *Well Gina, we haven't heard much from you. What do you think?*

GINA: *Well for one thing, my daughter got married against my advice. I don't think any woman should get married today until they pass the Equal Rights Amendment and it has been implemented. I think until we have a uniform marriage law; until we know the contract we are signing, you shouldn't live together.*

DR. DJERASSI: *Very interesting view, I haven't heard that one. Although it's an interesting one and I would tend to agree... uh, suppose the Equal Rights Amendment would pass, what then?*

GINA: *Well then you would have a reason for marrying.*

DR. DJERASSI: *And what is that?*

GINA: *Well if you were religious and wanted to make a contract—*

DR. DJERASSI: *Oh so you're putting religion into this?*

GINA: *When [my husband] and I lived together, we did not get married. But we did incorporate.*

DR. DJERASSI: *But you're talking on a religious basis for marriage.*

GINA: *Well I suppose that people who are religious want to get married.*

PAT: *But I think there's a matter of perceived security in marriage. I don't know why I would think that, because I certainly have not been secure in my marriages. However, I did say perceived.*

DR. DJERASSI: *Isn't that true of life? Everything is perception.*

PAT: *Yes, and I perceive it's time to say goodbye until next time, my friends.*

CHAPTER SIXTEEN

2013

What Not to Do: The Flatter than a Flitter Dinner

Hold on, darlin', if you think all my efforts at entertaining go smoothly, I'll give you a taste, a tiny one, of what a flatter-than-a-flitter Salon can be like. Not so long ago I threw a Roundtable supper where I learned, after all these years, what not following the rules could lead to; confusion and frustration.

Sean, my son, called me before coming to Los Angeles from his home in Brooklyn, suggesting putting together a Roundtable while he was here. He was excited to invite the famous Eve Martin. Eve Martin? Who was Eve Martin? The name did not resonate with me. Sean was certain that I knew the person. He repeated the name again and seemed happy for this guest to be a part of the Roundtable, that I asked him to spell it out. Steve Martin!

Oh, Steve Martin! Only the legendary comedian, writer, and actor. What a grand idea and excellent guest. It was a perfect fit. Sean said he would cook and host the supper. I could sit and enjoy the conversation and see what it's like to not be in charge for the first time.

When Steve arrived I met him at the door, welcomed him by saying, "You're Eve to me." And explained that I'm losing the "S" sounds, but Steve didn't laugh. Instead he showed me his hearing aid and said that he's losing the "s" sounds, too.

Sean is an excellent cook and proceeded to prepare a huge spread. He also insisted on having hors d'oeuvres. (Note: I never

GUESTS

Miranda July • Author, filmmaker, actor, and artist. Her films include *Me and You and Everyone We Know* and *The Future*. Her books include *The First Bad Man* and *No One Belongs Here More Than You: Stories*.

Mike Mills • Miranda July's husband and director of *Thumbsucker* and other films

Steve Martin • Author, comedian, actor, producer, and musician

Anne Stringfield • Steve Martin's wife and contributing writer to *The New Yorker*

Lisa Petrocelli • Writer, PR expert

Sean Wilsey • Author of *Oh the Glory of It All* and *More Curious*; editor-at-large for *McSweeny's Quarterly Concern* and son of Pat Montandon

Sammy Harkem • Editor of *Kramer's Ergot*; co-founder of Cinefamily; co-owner of Family Bookstore in Los Angeles

Mike White • Screenwriter of *Chuck & Buck, Nacho Libre,* and *School of Rock*; actor and producer

Sam Wasson • Author of *Fosse* and *A Splurch in the Kisser: The Movies of Blake Edwards*

serve hors d'oeuvres. A friend once said "I can't even get a peanut in your house before dinner." My answer and I still feel this way, was: *"Why would anyone want to eat before eating?"*

But, it's great to blame my son and not take responsibility myself. This is a Roundtable, food facilitates discussion and the conversation is what's important.

Sean continued cooking and made a special vegan meal for Mike White. With Sean switching from host to chef, I didn't know what to do. I had the Roundtable rules dialed in. They are important to me and I know how to run them to keep food and conversation flowing. The display of chef Sean made for a convoluted start that continued to unravel.

Also, generally, no couples are invited to the Roundtable. On the rare occasions that it happens, I seat the spouses apart from each other so they can talk freely with other guests.

Steve brought his wife, Anne Stringfield, Miranda July brought her husband, and one woman arrived with her child. The Roundtable isn't a forum for children because we lose the parent to the child. I want Roundtables to focus on frank, open, and adult discussions. Children are adorable, so everyone gets distracted. It was a lesson that confirmed the rules I have set forth for decades. No kids.

With the fiasco of the food orgy Sean created and couples mingling, the Roundtable started and Sean just sat there. He turned to me like I was the host. It was embarrassing and I didn't know what to do. What I should have done was announce that my son was the host, given him my silver bell, relaxed and enjoyed the company. Chaos ensued and I should have just jumped on the table, danced, and blown a trumpet because the absurdity levels were high.

I got caught up in doin' it my way. I tried to bring it to some level of cohesion. Sammy Harkim is a sweet man and he was in a heavy discussion with the person sitting next to him, so I tried to break that up and divert their attention to other guests. That didn't work. I let that go, I didn't want to become a reluctant dictator at something that was failing from the start.

It reminded me of the need for one person to be the conductor so all the instruments will be able to make beautiful music together and keep the conversation flowing and the food items yummy, but simple.

At this abysmal failure of conversation, Sean also cooked up a separate forest for Mike White who was a true blue Vegan. There wasn't the camaraderie that I have experienced at my hundreds of luncheons. The conversation was not flowing, darlin'. It was dyin'.

The baby began to cry, the mom made a fuss, too. The focus was on the food. I was uncomfortable, so how could my guests feel comfortable? Which is a reminder to keep the guest list to ten or less. Fourteen people at my table was four too many.

Sometimes a celebrity can intimidate other guests into silence. We read about them, see their films, read their books and whatever gossip is unfit to print, and we become tongue-tied. These celebrities can seem like Alien beings otherworldly and powerful, unless they make an effort to show warmth and their human side. Most do, I'm happy to say.

Failure is part of the process. Even if I had known that my son expected me to play hostess, this dinner might have been a disaster anyway. But, for sure, the guest list would have had more diversity and I would have known more about the people sitting at my table. But everything is a learning experience, one that allows us to grow and correct our mistakes in the future.

I wish you super success in how you go about creating your Roundtable Salons. If you fail, keep moving forward and try, try again. The rewards of bringing people together and creating conversations include long-lasting friendships that enrich our lives and feed our souls.

I hand the torch to you. And if Eve Martin happens to be on your guest list have a banjo handy. He is a stellar banjo player as well as an amazing talent in many fields, and a truly nice man.

CHAPTER SEVENTEEN

1979
The Question Was Change

The Macedoine of Fruit was as colorful as the flowers in the center of the table: cold and tartly sweet. I watched Merla Zellerbach sampling it across the table. With her long, black hair, vivid coloring, and sparkling eyes, she looked like a portrait that might have been titled, *"Woman with Never a Care."* One would not guess that she had been through a double mastectomy. Recently she had been researching reconstructive breast surgery. I asked her if she would tell us about it.

MERLA: *A while back an article came over the wire services about all the great new techniques in reconstructive surgery for mastectomy victims, saying that women no longer need to fear this operation because it's now possible to rebuild a wonderful breast. My own reaction, of course, was to find out more about it which I did. Well, it turns out that these operations are very risky and very, very expensive. It takes three or four operations to get any sort of results.*

PAT: *Even if they do it at the time the breast is removed?*

MERLA: *If they do it at the time the breast is removed, it's very dangerous because it can interfere with followup cancer treatments and any further monitoring for cancer. So I think reputable physicians aren't advising it even though others are doing it and encouraging it. I always bristle at the word* "mutilation" when used to describe a mastectomy. But some of the techniques used in reconstructive surgery might be called that. A very common one is taking the lips of the vagina to build the new areola and nipples on the breast. Or else they take the old nipple and graft it on the thigh. So you have to go around wearing a nipple on your thigh while you are waiting to have three more operations. These will cost up to around $20,000, and the outcome is very chancy.

PAT: You spoke of mastectomy victims.

MERLA: I was quoting. I am a victim of cancer. The mastectomy was what cured me. But this plastic surgeon I talked to used the world "cripple." "Do you want to go on being a breast cripple all your life?" he asked me. That's the way they push reconstructive surgery. But my main feeling is that it's wrong to tell women they should not fear mastectomy because they can have a new breast and go around looking as good as new. The results don't bear that

---

GUESTS

Merla Zellerbach • Columnist for the *San Francisco Chronicle* and author

Dr. Rollo May • Psychologist and author of *Love and Will*

Marcia Brandwynne • T.V. Anchor

Eldridge Cleaver • Co-founder of the Black Panther Party and author of *Soul on Ice*

Dr. Mimi Silbert • Psychologist and co-president of Delancey Street

Daphne Greene • Socialite

Father Miles Riley • San Francisco pastor

out. And, anyway, people should go to their doctors for the right reason, which is concern for their health.

MARCIA: I just had a scare with a lump. It turned out not to be anything, but there is that terrible fear when the doctor starts looking and touching. And my doctor said that a lot of women aren't really afraid of the cancer. They are basically afraid of their husbands.

MERLA: A lot of women won't go to a doctor even though they know there's a lump. They are afraid of the way the other person will react if they lost a breast.

DR. MAY: But they don't need the breast. The man needs it!

MERLA: This plastic surgeon said to me, "Let's face it. This is a breast oriented society." And he told me that one woman had declared, when told her cancer had spread, "If I've only five years to live, I want to live them as a woman!"

PAT: As if she wouldn't be a woman!

MERLA: So she spent those last precious years going through four or five dehumanizing surgical experiences.

PAT: I think what you have done by speaking out has been so helpful. You and Betty Ford and Shirley Temple Black and Happy Rockefeller and others prominent and not so prominent have opened up what was a taboo subject for much too long so that women know they're not alone when they go through this.

MARCIA: They're certainly not alone. It's one out of fifteen women.

PAT: Well, enough talk about surgery. I want to hear from Rollo. He made an exception coming to this luncheon before finishing his book. Mostly, he's being a recluse until the book is completed. Now I'm wondering if you're willing the talk about it, Rollo.

DR. MAY: Very willing because I think it's a very important book. I don't think it's going to receive very much attention, but sometimes a writer has to write what he must write whether anybody ever reads it or not. This is a book on the paradoxes of freedom. I happen to believe that freedom is basic to all other values. Because if you don't have freedom, any other values you have will be the result of conformity or apathy or whatever. They won't be values that come from you. This is what I am trying to write about. But I don't think people are ready to start from scratch, which is what we really have to do. They are bound up in the status quo. But I think we have to start thinking about what kind of a world we want to live in, what kind of people we want to be. This means starting at the bottom, which to my mind, is the concept of freedom, which we have so misused in this country. We think freedom is a property value, which is a great curse because it ought to be a human value. Eldridge, the way you were concerned about the women you raped does not surprise me at all. Each was a real woman. It was not a bunch of money. I happen to believe that our whole culture has to be reorganized on the assumption that property values are irrelevant. The one thing that is relevant is human life. We have to start thinking of quality, not quantity.

ELDRIDGE: What you're saying is earthquaking!

DR. MAY: I would be for throwing aside all property values. I think that's what we're going to have to do, sooner or later. I think there's going to be a guaranteed income. I think that by the year 2000, there will be no more money. It will all be done on credit. Then we can then we will have to begin thinking in terms of human values.

DR. SILBERT: In a sense, among ourselves at Delancey Street, we have no money. Everyone receives exactly the same things, although some are capable of working and others, while we train them, are incapable of producing anything. And some of these people, when they come to us, believe that the world consists of tricks and those who trick them off. And they've been doing the tricking off. Then we bring them into a situation where it

*doesn't matter. All the clawing for property and goods and money
and success is irrelevant. Then there are the most fascinating
developments. Big, huge guys cry over something that happened
with one of the little children. There is an incredible reservoir of
human emotion. And many of them thought they didn't have these
feelings that that was a sucker's approach to life.*

DR. MAY: *I wish we could very much enlarge Delancey Street. That,
to me, is a very significant myth if I may use the world myth as
meaning an eternal truth. It's a very important myth for the future.
But it's a small operation for 250 million people.*

I thought it was time to wind things up. I knew Marcia had to get
away soon to prepare for her evening news broadcast. So I announced that it was time for <u>The Question</u>. I asked Eldridge to answer it first.

PAT: *Eldridge, we've been discussing change today. Rollo is
predicting many changes. How do you feel that you have
changed?*

ELDRIDGE: *I've changed. I was a Marxist. I had rejected spiritual
values. But then I saw communism firsthand, the kind of system
that is based on the philosophy, and it made me recoil. So I had
to go back and take another look at theology. But I think the
important change came when I became a father. Because when I
saw my children with a combination of my features and my wife's
features, it really just blew away the orientation that I had that all
this was just an accident. I saw the design in nature, and I was
convinced there was a Creator. And other things happened after
that which resulted in my conversion experience.*

DR. MAY: *Where did that come from, or did it just come from your
inner life?*

ELDRIDGE: *Nobody was sitting down with me and trying to instruct me. I had this lawyer in Paris. He was a Protestant in a Catholic country, a spiritual man, but he didn't try to proselytize me or anything like that. I was just exposed to his values and his world. It was a bad time for me. I wanted to go home to the United States. Friends of mine got into power and I thought they would help me, but they didn't. The whole bottom of my world fell out. I went into a deep depression. I felt trapped. I had a wife and two children, and my children didn't even speak English. They were going to French schools and becoming little French fried people. One night on my balcony, I just caved in. This is down near Cannes on the Mediterranean coast. A lot of people ask me, like, were you drunk? Had you been smoking? I was not high on anything. I was looking at the moon, a full moon, and I saw these shadows on it. I saw myself, my own profile, on the moon. I had been thinking of killing myself. I had the pistol. And I wondered if what I was seeing was a sign that death was near. And then my image fell away, and on the moon I saw a procession of my heroes: Fidel Castro, Mao Tse Tung, Karl Marx, Frederick Engels. And then the image of Jesus Christ. That was an unwelcome image because I didn't have anything to do with him, you know? It was like the last straw. I started crying. Just gushing out, real violent. I was trembling, and I had the sense that my soul was trembling. I was down on my knees, hanging onto the rail. And then I ran inside for a Bible. And it was there, this book I never read. I found the Twenty-third Psalm, which I had learned as a child. But I didn't know where to find the Lord's Prayer. That's what happened. Okay? I went to bed thoroughly confused. But when I woke up in the morning, I saw my way back home. I saw this path of light that ran through a prison cell, and I knew that all I had to do was surrender and come back home. I didn't have to depend on politicians. I just had to surrender and everything was going to come out all right. And that's what I did.*

The intensity with which Eldridge had recounted his experience had rendered us all mute. I waited a bit before I asked Marcia for her answer to <u>The Question</u>.

MARCIA: *Change oh, yes. I think I am getting more mature and less judgmental. And I can now enjoy the wonderful freedom of making the choice of whom I want to be with and whom I don't. That's maturing. And now, if you want any news at five o'clock, I'm going to have to run. I've enjoyed it.*

After she left, the rest of us continued to sip our coffee. I asked Rollo to answer <u>The Question</u>.

DR. MAY: *I believe that each person has one duty, one function, and that is to live out his own inner integrity, to be as wholly as he can. Now this is never going to be done, but it can be approximated. I think I must be as honest as I can with whatever inner guidance I have, and this is the way I have felt more and more as I have gotten older. In this disintegrating society, I think we have to live, as we used to say in theology, prolepsis. Are you familiar with that expression? It means you take the future and you live with it as of now. I think our task, or my task, at least, is to live in terms of what I earlier called the "myths." That is, the truths of a new society, a new Renaissance I see coming about the year 2000 or a few years after that. Now I may be completely wrong, but I don't have a right to go around asking "Am I right or wrong?" I have the right only to ask "What is it that I am guided to do?" Let me do that with my full strength, and let the future worry about the future.*

PAT: *That really takes some mulling over for me.*

DAPHNE: *It did for you too, didn't it, Rollo?*

MERLA: *You spoke of disintegration, Rollo. I think I have to come to terms with disintegration in my own life because I sense a loss of idealism and naiveté in my life that we were talking about before. My father was a Rabbi, and I was brought up to believe that there was good in everybody and no such thing as an evil person. But experience has taught me otherwise. I do believe that people are evil. I used to speak out against capital punishment, but I would tend toward favoring capital punishment now. Because I just can't see any reason for Charles Manson or someone like that to go on living. I know this isn't "enlightened," but to answer* <u>The Question</u>*, it is the way I am changing.*

FR. MILES: *That is very provocative, Merla. But, to be fair and to answer* <u>The Question</u>*, the way I have changed is that I have come to grips with authority in my life. I have let go, progressively, of a series of authority figures because I have learned that it is too high a price to pay in terms of freedom. This is a very big change for me, one that I am still making. I've a long way to go.*

PAT: *What about you, Daphne?*

DAPHNE: *My turn? I don't know, Pat. I am really in the middle of an awful lot of change right now. I don't know what will happen, but it keeps happening. That's dramatically different from knowing exactly where you are going and what you are doing. Right now I'm dealing with frustration and trying to be quiet, and both are difficult. I don't think I can answer* <u>The Question</u>*.*

PAT: *It's not required. How about you, Mimi?*

DR. MIMI: *I grew up in this very poor, Jewish traditional family. But we felt rich. There were these huge amounts of love. Just gushes of love. And I thought it was my job to love everybody who hadn't had that. And I started working in prisons with victims and criminals, and I was trying to transfer love. Then I came to Delancey Street and lived with them. And I found out that they were really brutal and vicious. I still think that comes from* *being victimized. But I found out that you don't change lives with beautiful beliefs or your own great warmth. It just doesn't work. Oh, it worked for me! I felt wonderful about doing that. But the people to whom I gave felt the way I think people do on the receiving end: They felt rotten. So I had to stop depending on love and start using power and action. There was a personal price to pay, but I think my life counts for more now. I have more freedom to move, to take action, to affect change, which ultimately makes a difference for lots more people.*

DAPHNE: *That's called growing up, I think.*

PAT: *Well, I'm last, and I feel very much like Daphne. I've asked a question I can't answer. I feel that the people who say "Pat you haven't changed" could be right because I feel I've changed a lot and yet I haven't changed at all. I think that whatever I am, whatever I envision, whatever I dream to be has always been there. It's a process of evolution with me. I know that at the time I was called the "Jet-Set Queen." That was a label put on me by other people. Now those people look at me and say, "Oh, what you're doing today is so important and so good. You've changed!" But, I haven't. I've just been given the emotional and financial security to do things I couldn't do before, to show a different facet of myself.*

DR. MAY: *Pat, I wonder when you say you haven't changed. I didn't know you back in the old Jet-Set days, but I would swear that if we were to look into it, we would see a great deal of what you call evolution.*

PAT: *Perhaps I haven't made myself quite clear. There were no Jet-Set days. Except in the media.*

ELDRIDGE: *Yeah, there I was, always referred to as an ex-rapist.*

DAPHNE: *And I was a socialite. I grew to hate that word.*

ELDRIDGE: *What I wonder about; do all of you here know each other for years and years?*

PAT: *No, not at all. Daphne knew Rollo, but I didn't know Rollo or Daphne either. Merla and I have been friends for some time, but I didn't know Mimi until today, and I only recently met Miles and Marcia.*

ELDRIDGE: *I'm just struck by how concerned everybody is, you know? And how we can sit around a table like this and talk about change and so forth. It's really fulfilling.*

FR. MILES: *What that means, Eldridge, is that there are a whole lot of people like us who are longing for permission to talk and share and communicate at this level the intellectual, the emotional. What the Roundtable does is give us permission to be. It's your doing, Pat.*

We were on our feet. Miles clasped my hands. I said, "I can give everybody else permission because I've given myself permission." Miles understood. We said goodbye. The Roundtable was over. But not the change it had brought to my perception of life.

These gatherings of people from all walks of life, who shared their honest experiences and knowledge, had also given me, over the years, the equivalency of a Harvard education. In time I was able to use the knowledge and self-assurance gained from Round-table discussions into Halls of Power and substantive meetings with Heads of State in twenty-six countries. Never underestimate the impact of a good lunch, great conversation, and the friends you make along the way.

> *These gatherings of people from all walks of life, who shared their honest experiences and knowledge, had also given me, over the years, the equivalency of a Harvard education.*

ACKNOWLEDGMENTS

As readers know, it truly takes a village to write a book, in my case, a city. The inhabitants of that city—Amy M. Inouye, my incredible book designer, top notch author and editor Julia Scheeres, Everlyn Choi for photography, and master chef Keith Graber who kept me well fed and roly-poly.

And I especially want to thank the incredible guests I have hosted at my table for forty-five years, their honesty, humor, tears and permission to record them gives *Recipes for Conversation* a rare authenticity. These conversations came from a place deep inside, a secret place few reveal until given permission by equally candid listeners.

Please accept these revelations by illustrious people, those you read about, the celebrities from all genres, as well as those like you and me—being who they really are without pretense or guile. Enjoy, learn, give yourself permission to create the atmosphere of acceptance and sincerity at your own Roundtable, showering you in enlightenment, you will be glad you did. It's fun, darlin'.

Also By Pat Montandon

BOOKS

How to Be a Party Girl

The Intruders

Making Friends (the first Soviet/American co-publication)

Celebrities and Their Angels

Oh the Hell of It All (Hardcover)

Whispers from God: A Life Beyond Imaginings

(Paperback version of *Oh the Hell of It All*)

Peeing on Hot Coals

PLAYS

Patience Patient

Them Oklahoma Hills

Family Album

Dreams Notwithstanding

POETRY

Black Silence

Testosterone Drums

Tiananmen Square

DMZ

American Dream

Children of Chernobyl

Ghosts

Truth

CPSIA information can be obtained
at www.ICGtesting.com
Printed in the USA
LVHW111112220121
677169LV00008B/221

9 781087 930541